Concepts
for Today

Second Edition

Reading For Today SERIES, BOOK 4

LORRAINE C. SMITH
Adelphi University

NANCY NICI MARE
English Language Institute
Queens College
The City University of New York

THOMSON
™
HEINLE

Australia • Canada • Mexico • Singapore • United Kingdom • United States

THOMSON
HEINLE

Concepts for Today, Second Edition
Lorraine C. Smith and Nancy Nici Mare

Publisher, Adult and Academic ESL: *James W. Brown*
Senior Acquisitions Editor: *Sherrise Roehr*
Director of Development: *Anita Raducanu*
Development Editor: *Sarah Barnicle*
Assistant Editor: *Audra Longert*
Editorial Intern: *Sarah Bilodeau*
Senior Production Editor: *Maryellen E. Killeen*
Senior Marketing Manager: *Charlotte Sturdy*
Director, Global ESL Training & Development:
  Evelyn Nelson

Senior Print Buyer: *Mary Beth Hennebury*
Contributing Writer: *Barbara Gaffney*
Compositor: *Parkwood Composition Service*
Project Manager: *Hockett Editorial Service*
Photo Researcher: *Susan Van Etten*
Photography Manager: *Sheri Blaney*
Illustrator: *Glenn Reid*
Cover Designer: *Ha Ngyuen*
Text Designer: *Carole Rollins*
Printer: *Quebecor World*

Printed in the United States of America
1 2 3 4 5 6 7 8 9 10   06 05 04 03

For more information contact Heinle, 25 Thomson Place, Boston, Massachusetts 02210 USA, or you can visit our Internet site at http://www.heinle.com

For permission to use material from this text or product contact us:
Tel   1-800-730-2214
Fax   1-800-730-2215
Web   www.thomsonrights.com

Library of Congress Control Number   2003108819

ISBN   1-4130-0812-7
ISE ISBN   1-4130-0078-9

To our parents: Peg and Smitty; Anthony and Antoinette

ACKNOWLEDGMENTS

We are grateful to everyone at Heinle, especially to Sherrise Roehr for her continued support, to Sarah Barnicle for her keen eye and untiring efforts, and to Maryellen Killeen for her hard work. Special thanks also go to Rachel Youngman of Hockett Editorial Service for her diligence. As always, we are appreciative of the ongoing encouragement from our family and friends.

L.C.S. and N.N.M.

CONTENTS

Chs 2, 4, 8 not in 3rd ed (∿ tests ?)

Unit and Chapter	Reading Skills Focus	Structure Focus	Follow-up Skills Focus and Activities
Unit 1 Living in Society Chapter 1 **The Paradox of Happiness** *Page 2*	• Preview reading through title and prereading questions to activate background knowledge • Analyze reading through true/false, multiple choice, and short answer questions • Use context clues to understand and use vocabulary • Use dictionary entries to select synonyms and accurate definitions • Identify main ideas and details • Organize information using an outline • Use outline notes to recall and summarize information	• Change verbs to nouns by adding the suffixes: *-ance* and *-ence* or *-ion* and *-tion* • Correctly identify and use parts of speech: nouns and verbs • Use singular and plural nouns; use correct verb tenses in affirmative or negative form • *Critical Thinking :* Express opinions supported by examples; compare and contrast ideas	• *Writing:* Write an opinion composition with supporting examples; make a list; create a survey
Chapter 2 **Close to Home: Technological Advances Erode Barrier Between Work and Home** *Page 20*	• Preview reading through the illustration, title, and prereading questions to activate background knowledge • Analyze reading through true/false, multiple choice, and short answer questions • Use context clues to understand and use vocabulary • Use dictionary entries to select synonyms and accurate definitions • Scan for main ideas and skim article for details • Organize information into a flowchart • Use flowchart to recall and summarize information	• Change verbs to nouns by adding the suffixes: *-ion* and *-tion* • Correctly identify and use parts of speech: nouns and verbs • Use singular and plural nouns; use correct verb tenses in affirmative or negative form	• *Critical Thinking:* Identify and understand inference; support answers with examples • *Writing:* Write about advantages and disadvantages; make a list • *Discussion:* Assert opinion and support with examples; compare and discuss personal lists
Chapter 3 **The Birth-Order Myth** *Page 39*	• Preview reading through prereading questions to activate background knowledge • Analyze reading through true/false, multiple choice, and short answer questions • Use context clues to understand vocabulary and punctuation marks • Use dictionary entries to select synonyms and accurate definitions • Take notes from reading and organize information using an outline • Use outline to recall and summarize information	• Change verbs to nouns by adding the suffix: *-ment* • Change adjectives to nouns by removing final *-t* adding the ending: *-ce* • Correctly identify and use parts of speech: nouns, verbs, adjectives • Use correct noun and verb forms	• *Critical Thinking:* Identify and understand inference; express opinions supported with examples; draw conclusions • *Writing:* Write an opinion paragraph with examples; analyze and record results of a survey • *Discussion:* Compare opinions about advantages and disadvantages; conduct a survey and discuss results • *Listening and Viewing:* **CNN® Video Report: Hot Spots and Wireless Technology** • *Viewing and Research:* **InfoTrac® Search:** Notebook Computers

Contents

Unit and Chapter	Reading Skills Focus	Structure Focus	Follow-up Skills Focus and Activities
Unit 2 **Safety and Health** Chapter 4 **Why So Many More Americans Die in Fires** *Page 62*	• Preview reading through the title and prereading questions to activate background knowledge • Analyze reading through true/false, multiple choice, and short answer questions • Use context clues to understand vocabulary • Use dictionary entries to select synonyms and accurate definitions • Scan for details • Organize information using a chart • Use notes from chart to recall and summarize information	• Change adjectives to nouns by removing final -t adding the ending: -ce • Change adjectives to nouns by adding the suffix: -ity • Correctly identify and use parts of speech: nouns, verbs, adjectives • Use correct noun and verb forms	• *Critical Thinking:* Identify and understand inferences; express opinions supported with examples; draw conclusions; identify problems and create solutions • *Writing:* Write an opinion paragraph supported with examples; make lists; write examples of building codes and fire laws • *Discussion:* Discuss fire prevention; make decisions • *Viewing and Research:* **Internet Search:** Historical Fires
Chapter 5 **Acupuncture: The New Old Medicine** *Page 80*	• Preview reading through the illustration, title, and prereading questions to activate background knowledge • Analyze reading through true/false, multiple choice, and short answer questions • Use context clues to understand vocabulary • Use dictionary entries to select synonyms and accurate definitions • Scan for main idea and important details • Organize information using an outline • Use outline to recall and summarize information	• Change verbs to nouns by adding the suffixes: -ion and -tion • Change adjectives to adverbs by adding the suffix: -ly • Correctly identify and use parts of speech: nouns and verbs; adjectives and adverbs • Use singular or plural nouns; use correct verb tenses in affirmative or negative form	• *Critical Thinking:* Understand inference; identify author's opinion and tone; express opinions supported with examples; draw conclusions; identify problems and create solutions • *Discussion:* Explain or describe traditional medicine—uses and practices; compare traditional treatments • *Writing:* Write an opinion paragraph supported with examples; record individual and class lists
Chapter 6 **Highs and Lows in Self-Esteem** *Page 104*	• Preview reading through the illustration, title, chart, and questions to activate background knowledge • Analyze reading through true/false, multiple choice, and short answer questions • Use context clues to understand vocabulary • Use dictionary entries to select synonyms and accurate definitions • Scan for details • Take notes in a flowchart • Use notes to recall and summarize information	• Change verbs to nouns by adding the suffixes: -tion and -ion • Correctly identify and use parts of speech: nouns and verbs • Use singular and plural nouns; use correct verb tenses in affirmative or negative form	• *Critical Thinking:* Critique author's conclusions; draw separate conclusions; reflect on personal and social implications; create analogies • *Discussion:* Assert opinion; give advice; describe stages of self-esteem; make plans; generate solutions • *Writing:* Take notes; support opinions with examples; record group ideas in chart form • *Listening and Viewing:* **CNN® Video Report:** Holiday House Fires • *Viewing and Research:* **InfoTrac® Search:** Acupuncture

Unit and Chapter	Reading Skills Focus	Structure Focus	Follow-up Skills Focus and Activities
Unit 3 Government and Education Chapter 7 **The Federal System of Government** *Page 130*	• Preview reading through the pre-reading questions to activate background knowledge • Analyze reading through true/false, multiple choice, and short answer questions • Use context clues to understand vocabulary • Use dictionary entries to select synonyms and accurate definitions • Scan for main idea and important details • Organize information using an outline • Use outline to recall and summarize information	• Change verbs to nouns by adding the suffix: *-ment* • Change adjectives to nouns by removing final *-t* adding the ending: *-ce* • Correctly identify and use parts of speech: nouns and verbs • Use singular and plural nouns; use correct verb tenses in affirmative or negative form	• *Critical Thinking:* Make inferences; support ideas with examples • *Discussion:* Compare types of governments; explain a branch of the U.S. government; compare and contrast governments • *Writing:* Take notes during student discussions; fill out chart; describe a form of government • *Viewing and Research:* **Internet Search:** Forms of Government/ The Constitution
Chapter 8 **Too Soon Old, Too Late Wise** *Page 156*	• Preview reading through the illustration, title, and prereading questions to activate background knowledge • Analyze reading through true/false, multiple choice, and short answer questions • Use context clues to understand vocabulary • Use dictionary entries to select synonyms and accurate definitions • Scan for main ideas and details • Take notes in a flowchart • Use the notes to recall and summarize information	• Change adjectives to nouns by adding the suffix: *-ity* • Change verbs to nouns by adding the suffixes: *-ance* and *-ence* • Correctly identify and use parts of speech: nouns, verb, and adjectives • Use singular and plural nouns; use correct verb tenses in affirmative or negative form	• *Critical Thinking:* Make inferences about the reading; support opinions with examples; discuss author's perspective • *Discussion and Writing:* Describe person discussed in the reading; reflect on laws and support ideas with examples; write a position or argument composition
Chapter 9 **The Pursuit of Excellence** *Page 171*	• Preview reading through the title and prereading questions to activate background knowledge • Analyze reading through true/false, multiple choice, and short answer questions • Use context clues to understand vocabulary • Use dictionary entries to select synonyms and accurate definitions • Scan for main ideas and details • Organize information using a chart • Use chart to recall and summarize information	• Change adjectives to nouns by adding the suffix: *-ity* • Change adjectives to nouns by removing final *-t* adding the ending: *-ce* • Correctly identify and use parts of speech: adjectives, nouns and verbs • *Listening and Viewing:* **CNN®** **Video Report:** Vanishing Retirement • *Viewing and Research:* **InfoTrac® Search:** Foreign Students in the United States	• *Critical Thinking:* Make inferences; make reasonable assumptions; analyze author's attitude and purpose • *Discussion:* Conduct survey and analyze resulting data; plan strategies; discuss advantages and disadvantages; make rules in group and present to class • *Writing:* Use examples from reading to support opinion; in a chart compare and contrast advantages and disadvantages; describe an experience; make a list; write a letter

Unit and Chapter	Reading Skills Focus	Structure Focus	Follow-up Skills Focus and Activities
Unit 4 **Science and Technology** Chapter 10 **Antarctica: Whose Continent Is It Anyway?** *Page 198*	• Preview illustration, title, and pre-reading questions to activate background knowledge • Analyze reading through true/false, multiple choice, and short answer questions • Use context clues to understand vocabulary • Use dictionary entries to select synonyms and accurate definitions • Scan reading for main ideas and details • Take notes and organize information using an outline • Use outline to recall and summarize information	• Change verbs to nouns by adding the suffix: *-ment* • Change verbs to nouns by adding the suffixes: *-tion* and *-ion* • Correctly identify and use parts of speech: nouns and verbs • Use singular and plural noun forms; use correct verb tenses in affirmative or negative form	• *Critical Thinking:* • *Discussion:* Compare ideas; discuss rules; discuss places of interest to tourists • *Writing:* Make a list of group opinions; write guidelines; write a composition explaining your opinion; write a descriptive journal entry • *Viewing and Research:* **Internet Search:** Antarctica
Chapter 11 **A Messenger from the Past** *Page 215*	• Preview illustration, title, and pre-reading questions to activate background knowledge • Analyze reading through true/false, multiple choice, and short answer questions • Use context clues to understand vocabulary • Use dictionary entries to select synonyms and accurate definitions • Scan for main ideas and details • Take notes in a flowchart • Use notes to recall and summarize information	• Change verbs to nouns by adding the suffixes: *-tion* and *-ion* • Correctly identify and use parts of speech: nouns and verbs • Use singular and plural noun forms; use correct verb tenses in affirmative or negative form	• *Critical Thinking:* Analyze the author's tone and purpose; understand the feeling of the reading; support opinion with examples; make inferences • *Discussion:* Compare lists of questions • *Writing:* Write a descriptive journal entry about an imagined historical scene; make a list of questions • *Viewing and Research:* **Internet Search:** Ice Man of Tyrol
Chapter 12 **Is Time Travel Possible?** *Page 235*	• Preview illustration, title, and pre-reading questions, take a survey, and fill out chart to activate background knowledge • Analyze reading through true/false, multiple choice, and short answer questions • Use context clues to understand vocabulary • Use dictionary entries to select synonyms and accurate definitions • Scan reading for the main idea • Organize information using a table or chart • Use a table or chart to recall and summarize information	• Change verbs to nouns by adding the suffix: *-al* • Correctly identify and use parts of speech: adjectives, nouns, and verbs • Use correct verb tenses in affirmative or negative form	• *Critical Thinking:* Analyze a proverb; support opinions with examples; speculate on reasons for results of survey • *Discussion:* Discuss, conduct, and analyze results of the Time Preference Survey • *Writing:* Write a descriptive composition about the following: an imaginary meeting, a change in history, the future, and time travel • *Listening and Viewing:* **CNN®Video Report:** Antarctica's Future • *Viewing and Research:* **InfoTrac® Search:** Ice Man of Tyrol

PREFACE

Concepts for Today, Second Edition, is a reading skills text intended for high-intermediate, college-bound students of English as a second or foreign language. The passages in this book have been selected from original articles published in a wide variety of periodicals and newspapers, thus allowing students the opportunity to read authentic materials from American publications. As they engage with the materials in each chapter of this book, students develop the kinds of extensive and intensive reading skills they will need to achieve academic success in English.

Concepts for Today, Second Edition, is one in a series of five reading skills texts. The complete series has been designed to meet the needs of students from the beginning to the advanced levels and includes the following:

- *Themes for Today, 2e ...*   beginning
- *Insights for Today, 3e ...*   high beginning
- *Issues for Today, 3e ...*   intermediate
- *Concepts for Today, 2e ...*   high intermediate
- *Topics for Today, 3e ...*   advanced

Concepts for Today, Second Edition, provides students with essential practice in the types of reading skills they will need in an academic environment. It requires students not only to read text, but also to examine information from various forms of charts, illustrations, and photographs. Furthermore, students are given the opportunity to speak and write about their own experiences, countries, and cultures in English and to compare these experiences and ideas with those of people from the United States and other countries.

This thematically organized text consists of four units, each containing three chapters that deal with related subjects. This organization provides for a natural recycling of content-specific vocabulary and concepts and discipline-specific sentence structure and rhetorical patterns. It should be noted that although all three chapters in each unit are linked by theme, they can as easily be taught individually as in concert with one another. For the instructor who chooses to teach all three chapters in each unit, there is a unit-ending crossword puzzle and a discussion section that tie together the three related topics.

The initial exercise preceding each reading encourages the students to think about the ideas, facts, and vocabulary that will be presented in the passage. Discussing unit and chapter illustrations in class helps students visualize what they are going to read about and gives them cues for the new vocabulary they will encounter. The exercises that follow the reading passage are intended to develop and improve reading proficiency, including the ability to learn new vocabulary from context and to develop comprehension of English sentence structure, and study skills such as note-taking and proper dictionary use. The follow-up activities give students the opportunity to master useful vocabulary encountered in the articles through discussion and group work and lead the students to a comprehension of main ideas and specific information.

New to the Second Edition

While most reading topics and activities in *Concepts for Today, Second Edition*, remain from the previous edition, the authors have made some important changes to this edition. The second edition contains two new chapters: "Close to Home: Technological Advances Erode Barrier Between Work and Home" in the Living in Society unit and "Highs and Lows in Self-Esteem" in the Safety and Health unit.

In addition to the new chapters, the second edition is now accompanied by audiocassettes or audio CDs on which all the readings are recorded, as well as a CNN® videotape composed of authentic news reports, which complement the topic of a chapter in each unit. Video previewing, viewing, and post-viewing activities are found at the end of each unit to help students better enjoy and learn from the video clips. Also found at the end of each unit and new to *Concepts for Today, Second Edition,* are InfoTrac® research activities that replace the Library Mastery Research sections. These activities are designed to encourage students with school or personal access to the Internet to research more about topics they've encountered in the text. All the activities are presented to prepare students for academic work and the world of information they will encounter.

These revisions and enhancements to *Concepts for Today, Second Edition,* have been designed to help students improve their reading skills and develop confidence as they work through the text. At the same time the second edition is structured so that teachers can observe students steadily progressing toward skillful, independent reading.

INTRODUCTION

How to Use This Book

Every chapter in this book consists of the following:

Prereading Preparation
Reading Passages
Fact-Finding Scanning Exercise
Reading Analysis
Word Forms Exercise
Dictionary Skills
Information Organization
Information Organization Quiz and Summary
Critical Thinking Strategies
Follow-up Discussion and Writing Activities
Cloze Quiz

In order to get the students out of the classroom and give them the chance to use English in the real world, there are surveys in the follow-up activities section of several chapters. Each unit contains a crossword puzzle and unit discussion questions. The crossword puzzle incorporates vocabulary from all three chapters in the unit. The discussion section at the end of each unit ties in the related topics of the three chapters. CNN video and InfoTrac® research activities using unit topics are found on the final page of each unit.

The format of the chapters in the book is consistent. Although each chapter can be done entirely in class, some exercises may be assigned for homework. This, of course, depends on the individual teacher's preference, as well as the availability of class time.

Prereading Preparation

The prereading activity is designed to stimulate student interest and provide preliminary vocabulary for the passage itself. The importance of prereading preparation should not be underestimated. Studies have shown the positive effect of prereading preparation in motivating student interest, activating background knowledge, and enhancing reading comprehension. Time should be spent describing and discussing both unit and chapter photographs and illustrations as well as discussing the title and the prereading questions. Furthermore, the students should try to relate the topic to their own experiences and try to predict what they are going to read about.

The Reading Passage

As the students read the passage for the first time, they should be encouraged to read *ideas.* In English, ideas are in groups of words in sentences and in paragraphs, not in individual words.

Fact-Finding Scanning Exercise

After the first reading, students will read the True/False statements, then go back to the passage and scan for the information that will clarify whether each statement is true or false. If the statement is false, the students will rewrite the statement so that it becomes true. This activity can be done individually or in groups.

Reading Analysis

The students will read each question and answer it. This exercise deals with vocabulary from context, transition words, punctuation clues, sentence structure, sentence comprehension, and pronoun referents. The teacher should review personal and relative pronouns before doing this section. This exercise may be assigned for homework, or it may be done in class individually or in groups, giving the students the opportunity to discuss their reasons for their answers.

Word Form Exercise

As an introduction to the word form exercises in this book, it is recommended that the teacher first review parts of speech, especially verbs, nouns, adjectives, and adverbs. Teachers should point out each word form's position in a sentence.

Students will develop a sense for which part of speech is missing in a given sentence. Teachers should also point out clues to tense and number, and to whether an idea is affirmative or negative. The teacher can do the first item as an example with the students before the exercise. Each section has its own instructions, depending on the particular pattern that is being introduced. For example, in the section containing words which take *-tion* in the noun form, the teacher can explain that in this exercise the student will look at the two types of words that use the suffixes *-ion* or *-tion* in their noun form. (1) Some words simply add *-ion* to the verb: *suggest/suggestion*; if the word ends in *-e*, the *-e* is dropped first, and *-tion* is added: *produce/production*; (2) other words drop the final *-e* and add *-ation: examine/ examination*. This exercise is very effective when done in pairs. After students have a working knowledge of this type of exercise, it can be assigned for homework.

Dictionary Skills

This exercise provides students with much needed practice in selecting the appropriate dictionary entry for an unknown word, depending on the context. In each of the first six chapters, the students are given entries from *Heinle's Newbury House Dictionary* for several words from the reading in that chapter. The sentence containing the dictionary word is provided below the entry. The student selects the appropriate entry and writes the entry number and the definition or synonym into the sentence in the space provided. The students should write the answer in a grammatically correct form, since they may not always copy verbatim from the dictionary. In Chapters 7 to 12, the format is the same, but the entries are from *Merriam-Webster's Online Dictionary*. The students can work in pairs on this exercise and report back to the class. They should be prepared to justify their choices.

Information Organization

In this exercise, students are asked to read the passage a second time, take notes, and organize the information they have just read. They may be asked to complete an outline, a table, or a flowchart. The teacher may want to review the concept of note-taking before beginning the exercise. The outline, table, or flowchart can be sketched on the blackboard by the teacher or a student and completed by individual students in front of the class. Variations can be discussed by the class as a group. It should be pointed out to the students that in American colleges, teachers often base their exams on the notes that students are expected to take during class lectures and that they, too, will be tested on *their* notes.

Information Organization Quiz and Summary

This quiz is based on the notes the students took in the Information Organization exercise. Students should be instructed to read the questions and then refer to their notes to answer them. They are also asked to write a summary of the article. The teacher may want to review how to summarize. This section can be a written assignment to be done as homework or as an actual test. Alternately, it can be prepared in class and discussed.

Critical Thinking Strategies

The students refer back to parts of the article and think about the implications of the information or comments it contains. There are also questions about the author's purpose and tone. The goal of the exercise is for students to form their own ideas and opinions on aspects of the topic discussed. The students can work on these questions as individual writing exercises or in a small group discussion activity.

Follow-up Discussion and Writing Activities

This section contains various activities appropriate to the information in the passages. Some activities are designed for pair and small-group work. Students are encouraged to use the information and vocabulary from the passages both orally and in writing. The teacher may also use these questions and activities as homework or in-class assignments. There is a **Write in Your Journal** suggestion for every chapter, and students should be encouraged to keep a journal. Instructors should respond to the students' journal entries, but not correct them.

Cloze Quiz

The Cloze quiz is a section of the passage itself, but with words missing. The Cloze quiz tests not only vocabulary, but also sentence structure and general comprehension. The students are given the missing words that are to be filled in the blank spaces. The quiz is placed at the end of each chapter. The quizzes can be done either as a test or as a group assignment.

CNN® Video Report and InfoTrac® College Edition Research

On the final page of each unit are optional activities designed to accompany one or two of the topics presented in each unit. Authentic CNN videos were chosen to expand on concepts presented in the readings, to reinforce vocabulary learned, and to encourage individual interest as well as group discussion.

Each unit also includes a research activity that asks student to investigate a chapter topic more deeply, using InfoTrac College Edition. InfoTrac is an online library that stores 10,000,000 articles, accesses 4,000 journals, and is free to students using *Concepts for Today, Second Edition*. Using individual passwords, students can access this electronic library of academic information on the Internet—free for four months.

Index of Key Words and Phrases

This section contains words and phrases from all the chapters for easy reference. It is located after the last chapter.

Skills Chart and Skills Index

These sections contain lists of skill areas encountered in each chapter and throughout the book. These will be helpful resources for teachers addressing national and state standards as well as their own program goals and skill objectives.

UNIT 1

LIVING IN SOCIETY

The Paradox of Happiness
by Diane Swanbrow
Psychology Today

Prereading Preparation

1. a. In groups of three, write a definition of **happy.** Write what it means to be happy. On the blackboard, compare your definitions with the definitions of the other groups in the class.
    b. Do the same for **unhappy.**
    c. Compare your class explanations of **happy** and **unhappy.** Are they opposites? Is there a relationship between happiness and unhappiness?

2. What makes you happy? When do you feel happy?

3. What makes you feel unhappy?

4. a. Are you a happy person?
    b. Do you come from a happy family?

5. Do you think your environment can cause you to be happy or unhappy? Explain your answer.

6. Look at the title of this article. What is a **paradox?** Why might there be a paradox involving happiness and unhappiness?

The Paradox of Happiness

It's plain common sense—the more happiness you feel, the less unhappiness you experience. It's plain common sense, but it's not true. Recent research reveals that happiness and unhappiness are not really flip sides of the same emotion. They are two distinct feelings that, coexisting, rise and fall independently.

"You'd think that the higher a person's level of unhappiness, the lower their level of happiness and vice versa," says Edward Diener, a University of Illinois professor of psychology who has done much of the new work on positive and negative emotions. But when Diener and other researchers measure people's average levels of happiness and unhappiness, they often find little relationship between the two.

The recognition that feelings of happiness and unhappiness can coexist much like love and hate in a close relationship may offer valuable clues on how to lead a happier life. It suggests, for example, that changing or avoiding things that make you miserable may well make you less miserable but probably won't make you any happier. That advice is backed up by an extraordinary series of studies which indicate that a genetic predisposition for unhappiness may run in certain families. On the other hand, researchers have found, happiness doesn't appear to be anyone's heritage. The capacity for joy is a talent you develop largely for yourself.

Psychologists have settled on a working definition of the feeling— happiness is a sense of subjective well-being. They've also begun to find out who's happy, who isn't, and why. To date, the research hasn't found a simple recipe for a happy life, but it has discovered some of the actions and attitudes that seem to bring people closer to that most desired of feelings.

In a number of studies of identical and fraternal twins, researchers have examined the role genetics plays in happiness and unhappiness. The work suggests that although no one is really born to be happy, sadness may run in families.

In one University of Southern California study, psychologist Laura Baker and colleagues compared 899 individuals who had taken several commonly used tests for happiness and unhappiness. The men and women included 105 pairs of identical and fraternal twins as well as grandparents, parents and young adult offspring from more than 200 other families.

"Family members," Baker reports, "resembled each other more in their levels of unhappiness than in their levels of happiness." Furthermore, identical twins were much closer than fraternal twins in unhappiness, a finding that implies a genetic component.

39	In a study at the University of Minnesota, twins (some raised
40	together and others who had grown up apart) were tested for a wide range
41	of personality traits. In terms of happiness—defined as the capacity to enjoy
42	life—identical twins who were separated soon after birth were considerably
43	less alike than twins raised together. But when it came to *unhappiness,* the
44	twins raised apart—some without contact for as long as 64 years—were as
45	similar as those who'd grown up together.
46	Why is unhappiness less influenced by environment? When we're
47	happy we are more responsive to people and keep up connections better than
48	when we're feeling sad.
49	This doesn't mean, however, that some people are born to be sad and
50	that's that. Genes may predispose one to unhappiness, but disposition can
51	be influenced by personal choice. You can increase your happiness through
52	your own actions.
53	In a series of experiments by psychologists John Reich and Alex
54	Zautra at Arizona State University, they asked students to select their
55	favorite activities from a list of everyday pleasures—things like going to a
56	movie, talking with friends and playing cards.
57	Then the researchers instructed some of the subjects to increase the
58	number of favorite activities they participated in for one month (the other
59	participants in the study served as controls and did not vary their activity
60	level). Results: Those who did more of the things they enjoyed were happier
61	than those who didn't. The conclusion, then, is that the pleasure we get from
62	life is largely ours to control.

Fact-Finding Exercise

Read the passage once. Then read the following statements. Scan the article quickly to find out if each statement is true (T) or false (F). If a statement is false, change it so that is is true.

1. _____ T _____ F   The feeling of unhappiness may be genetic.

   _____

2. _____ T _____ F   There is a strong relationship between levels of happiness and unhappiness in a person.

   _____

3. _____ T _____ F   Researchers have found that happiness is inherited.

   _____

4. _____ T _____ F   Unhappiness is less influenced by environment than it is by genetics.

   _____

5. _____ T _____ F   It is impossible to increase your happiness.

   _____

6. _____ T _____ F   We can control our own happiness.

   _____

Read each question carefully. Circle the number or letter of the correct answer, or write your answer in the space provided.

1. Read lines 6 and 7: "You'd think that the higher a person's level of unhappiness, the lower their level of happiness and **vice versa.**"
   a. **Vice versa** means that
      1. the lower a person's level of unhappiness, the higher their level of happiness
      2. the higher a person's level of unhappiness, the higher their level of happiness
      3. the lower a person's level of unhappiness, the lower their level of happiness
   b. **Vice versa** means
      1. the same thing is true
      2. the reverse is true

2. Read lines 9–11. What does **the two** refer to?
   a. Diener and other researchers
   b. Positive and negative emotions
   c. Happiness and unhappiness

3. Read lines 14–16. **Miserable** means

   _____

4. Read lines 16–19.
   a. What does **back up** mean?
      1. Go behind
      2. Write
      3. Support
   b. "Studies indicate that a genetic predisposition for unhappiness may run in certain families. **On the other hand,** happiness doesn't appear to be anyone's heritage." This sentences means that
      1. the tendency to be unhappy is inherited, but happiness is not
      2. the tendency to be unhappy is inherited, and happiness is, too
      3. the tendency to be happy is inherited, but unhappiness is not

c. Complete the following sentence with the appropriate choice:
John is happy being a student in another country because he can study what he wants. **On the other hand,** he is unhappy because
   1. he is far from his family and friends
   2. he knows people from many different countries
   3. his English skills are improving

5. Read lines 39–45.
   a. According to the University of Minnesota study, what is happiness?

   _____

   b. How do you know?

   _____

   c. Why is the phrase **some without contact for as long as 64 years** separated from the rest of the sentence by dashes (—)?

   _____

6. Read lines 49–50. **That's that** means:
   a. some people are born to be sad, and there is nothing they can do to change the situation
   b. some people are born to be sad, and they don't think about it
   c. some people are born to be sad, and some people are born to be happy

7. Read lines 53–56.
   a. What are some of the everyday pleasures on the list that the students read?

   _____

   b. How do you know?

   _____

8. Read lines 60–62.
   a. **Those who didn't** refers to
      1. the students who didn't participate in the study
      2. the students who didn't increase the number of favorite activities
      3. the students who didn't become happier
   b. In this context, **largely** means
      1. hugely
      2. completely
      3. mostly

C. Word Forms

Part 1

In English, verbs can change to nouns in several ways. Some verbs become nouns by adding the suffixes *-ance* or *-ence,* for example, *insist (v.), insistence (n.).*

Complete each sentence with the correct form of the words on the left. **Use the simple present tense of the verbs, in either the affirmative or the negative form. Use the singular form of the nouns.**

appear *(v.)*
appearance *(n)*

1. a. Peter _____ to be very unhappy.
   b. His sad _____ makes me wonder what's wrong.

avoid *(v.)*
avoidance *(n.)*

2. a. Susan always _____ going to a doctor even when she's very sick.
   b. Her _____ of doctors is not a good idea. She should see one when she's ill.

exist *(v.)*
existence *(n.)*

3. a. Some people believe in the _____ of life in other solar systems.
   b. I also think that life _____ on other planets besides Earth.

resemble *(v.)*
resemblance *(n.)*

4. a. Michael _____ his mother at all. She has blonde hair and blue eyes. He has dark hair and brown eyes.
   b. Michael has a much stronger _____ to his father, who has dark hair and eyes, too.

assist *(v)*
assistance *(n.)*

5. a. Can you help me for a moment? I need your _____. This box is too heavy for me to pick up.
   b. If you _____ me, I won't be able to pick up the box.

perform *(v.)*
performance *(n.)*

6. a. The actor in the new play _____ very well in all his appearances.
   b. Consequently, I am looking forward to his first _____ tonight.

In English, verbs can change to nouns in several ways. Some verbs become nouns by adding the suffixes *-ion* or *-tion,* for example, *suggest (v.), suggestion (n.).*

Complete each sentence with the correct form of the words on the left. Be careful of spelling changes. **Use the simple present tense of the verbs, in the affirmative form. Use the singular form of the nouns.**

indicate *(v.)*
indication *(n.)*

1. a. Traffic signals have three signals. A red light _____ "stop," and a green light means "go."
   b. A yellow, or amber, light is an _____ that the light is going to become red. It means "prepare to stop."

participate *(v.)*
participation *(n.)*

2. a. Many college students _____ in sports such as soccer, tennis, and swimming to keep in shape.
   b. In fact, regular _____ in a sport is also a good way to make friends.

define *(v.)*
definition *(n.)*

3. a. I don't understand what *influence* means. Can you give me a simple _____?
   b. Most people _____ *influence* as the power to affect a person or an event.

recognize *(v.)*
recognition *(n.)*

4. a. Joan has an incredible memory for faces. She actually _____ people that she hasn't seen for years.
   b. Her powers of _____ are well known among her friends.

imply *(v.)*
implication *(n.)*

5. a. Diane Swanbrow _____ that many "opposite" feelings may not really be opposites at all.
   b. This is an interesting _____. Are *like* and *dislike* not really opposites?

D. DICTIONARY SKILLS

Read the dictionary entry for each word. Choose the appropriate definition. Then write the number and the synonym or meaning in the space provided. The first one has been done as an example.

1.
> **recognition** *n* **1** recognizing or being recognized: *Recognition of the new state is unlikely,* it is unlikely that diplomatic relations will be established with it. **2** acknowledgment. **3** favorable attention or notice.

The _(2) acknowledgment_ that feelings of happiness and unhappiness can coexist may offer clues to a happier life.

2.
> **close** *adj* **1** near (in space or time): *fire a gun at ~ range.* **2** with little or no space in between: *The soldiers advanced in ~ order,* with little space between them. **3** strict; severe. **4** thorough: *paid ~ attention.* **5** intimate: *a ~ friend/friendship.* **6** nearly even; almost equal: *a ~ contest/election.* **7** (of the weather or air) uncomfortably heavy.

Feelings of love and hate can coexist in relationships that are very (___)_____, for example, the relationship between a husband and wife.

3.
> **lead** *v* **1** guide or take, esp by going in front. **2** guide the movement of (a person, etc) by the hand, by touching him, or by a rope, etc: *~ a blind man/a horse.* **3** act as head; direct; manage. **4** have the first place in; go first. **5** guide the actions and opinions of; influence; persuade. **6** (cause a person to) pass, spend (his life, etc): *~ a miserable existence.* **7** make the first move.

Understanding our feelings helps us (___)_____ lives that are happier.

4.

| disposition *n* **1** arrangement (the more usual word): *the ~ of furniture in a room.* **2** a person's natural qualities of mind and character: *a man with a cheerful ~.* **3** power of ordering and disposing: *Who has the ~ of his property,* the power or authority to dispose of it? |

(___) _____ can be influenced by personal choice. In other words, you can increase your happiness through your own actions.

Read the article a second time. Underline what you think are the main ideas. Then scan the article and complete the following outline, using the sentences that you have underlined to help you. You will use this outline later to answer specific questions about the article.

I.   What New Research Shows About Happiness and Unhappiness
   A. The tendency to feel unhappy may be in your genes
   B.
   C.

II. Studies on the Role of Genetics in Happiness and Unhappiness
   A. University of Southern California
      1. subjects: 899 individuals (identical and fraternal twins, grandparents, parents, and young adult offspring)
      2. results:
      3. conclusion:
   B. University of Minnesota
      1. subjects:
      2. results:
         a. in terms of happiness,
         b. in terms of unhappiness,
      3. conclusion:

III. The Implications of the Studies on Happiness and Unhappiness
   A. Genes only predispose a person to unhappiness
   B.

IV. Arizona State University Experiment on Happiness
   A. subjects:
   B. experiment:
      1.
      2.
   C. result:
   D. conclusion: the pleasure we get from life is largely ours to control

Information Organization Quiz and Summary

Read each question carefully. Use your notes to answer the questions. Do not refer back to the text. Write your answers in the space provided under each question. When you are finished, write a brief summary of the article.

1. What do researchers believe about happiness and unhappiness?

    _____

    _____

    _____

2. Describe the study done at the University of Southern California. Who did researchers study? What did the researchers learn?

    _____

    _____

    _____

3. Describe the experiment done at Arizona State University. Who did the researchers study? How? What was the result of the study?

    _____

    _____

    _____

4. According to this article, how can we increase our happiness?

    _____

    _____

    _____

Summary

_____

_____

_____

_____

_____

G. *Critical Thinking Strategies*

Read each question carefully. Write your response in the space provided. Remember that there is no one correct answer. Your response depends on what **you** think.

1. According to this article, feelings of happiness and unhappiness can coexist. Similarly, love and hate can coexist in a close relationship. How can you explain such conflicting feelings in a relationship? Do you think a person can be happy and sad at the same time? Explain your answer.

   _____

   _____

   _____

   _____

2. The author mentions several studies of identical and fraternal twins. These studies conclude that sadness may run in families. Why do you think researchers like to study twins rather than other brothers and sisters? Why do you think researchers compare identical twins who grew up together with identical twins who grew up apart?

   _____

   _____

   _____

   _____

3. According to the University of Southern California study, "identical twins were much closer than fraternal twins in unhappiness, a finding that implies a genetic component." Why do you think identical twins were more alike than fraternal twins were?

   _____

   _____

   _____

   _____

4. The author describes two studies, one at the University of Southern California and one at the University of Minnesota. She also describes an experiment at Arizona State University. What do you think is the difference between doing a study and doing an experiment?

_____

_____

_____

_____

5. What do you think the author believes about happiness and unhappiness? Does she believe they are opposites? What do you think her opinion is?

_____

_____

_____

_____

H. *Follow-up Discussion* AND *Writing Activities*

1. According to the author, Diane Swanbrow, there are seven steps to happiness:

   1. Develop loving relationships with other people.
   2. Work hard at what you like.
   3. Be helpful to other people.
   4. Make the time to do whatever makes you happy.
   5. Stay in good physical condition.
   6. Be organized, but be flexible in case something unexpected comes up.
   7. Try to keep things in perspective.

   Alone, or with a classmate, examine these seven steps. Put them in order of importance to you. For example, the most important step to happiness is number one; the least important step is number seven. Compare your ordered list with your classmates' lists.

2. Work with your classmates as a group.

   a. Make a list of activities that people enjoy (e.g., going to the movies, listening to music, etc.).
   b. Take a survey to see which activities each classmate enjoys. Write the results on the blackboard.
   c. Refer to the Activity Chart on page 18. Add to the chart the activities that you listed on the board. Keep a personal record of the activities you do for the rest of the term. Use each box on the right for a weekly check.
   d. At the end of the term, do an in-class survey to find out if the people who increased the number of favorite activities that they participated in actually feel happier.
   e. Do your results support or disprove the Arizona State University findings?

3. **Write in your journal.** Researchers think that sadness runs in families. Do you agree or disagree? Write a composition explaining your opinion. Give examples to support your ideas.

ACTIVITY CHART

Activity \ Week									
read									
watch TV									
write letters									
listen to music									
take a walk									
go bicycling									

Cloze Quiz

Chapter 1: The Paradox of Happiness

Read the passage on this page. Fill in the blanks with one word from the list. Use each word only once.

advice	emotions	higher	level	researchers
appear	found	joy	miserable	run
avoiding	genetic	largely	recognition	studies
close	happier	less	relationship	unhappiness

"You'd think that the _____ a person's level of unhappiness, the lower
                              (1)
their _____ of happiness and vice versa," says Edward Diener, who has done
       (2)
much of the new work on positive and negative _____. But when Diener and
                                                      (3)
other _____ measure people's average levels of happiness and unhappiness,
       (4)
they often find little _____ between the two.
                           (5)
        The _____ that feelings of happiness and _____ can coex-
             (6)   (7)
ist much like love and hate in a _____ relationship may offer valuable clues on
                                     (8)
how to lead a _____ life. It suggests, for example, that changing or
               (9)
_____ things that make you _____ may well make you
       (10)   (11)
_____ miserable but probably won't make you any happier. That
       (12)
_____ is backed up by an extraordinary series of _____ which
       (13)   (14)
indicate that a _____ predisposition for unhappiness may _____
                  (15)   (16)
in certain families. On the other hand, researchers have _____, happiness
                                                              (17)
doesn't _____ to be anyone's heritage. The capacity for _____ is a
          (18)   (19)
talent you develop _____ for yourself.
                      (20)

Close to Home:
Technological Advances Erode Barrier Between Work and Home
by Veronica James
The Los Angeles Times

Prereading Preparation

1. Look at the photograph. Describe what the man is doing in the photo. Where is he?

2. a. Many different kinds of modern technology are used in the workplace to help workers stay in contact with their jobs, even when they are at home. Work with a partner. Make a list of examples of this kind of technology.

Examples of Modern Technology	
1.	4.
2.	5.
3.	6.

b. It is important for some workers to stay in contact with their jobs at all times. What are some examples of these types of jobs? Make a list.

Examples of Jobs	
1.	4.
2.	5.
3.	6.

3. What are some reasons why workers might need to be in contact with their jobs at all times? Discuss them with your classmates.

4. Read the title and subtitle of this chapter. What do you think this article will be about?

Close to Home

1   Some people can never get away from work these days. They're at the
2   constant mercy of their cell phones, pagers, two-way radios, or other electronic
3   devices. Take my sister Cindy. When it comes to high-tech gadgets, she was
4   ahead of her time. Twenty years ago her business phone rang at home and an
5   ever-present walkie-talkie was there to provide access and communication
6   among her husband, herself, and the truck drivers in their small business. Her
7   husband was one of the first people I knew with a cell phone, back when they
8   were known as "car phones" because they didn't detach from the car.
9   Cindy recalls attending her kids' soccer games with an oversized walkie-
10 talkie in hand, so she could conduct business, if necessary. Today, the company
11 is equipped with cell phones, two-way radios, and all-in-one radio and
12 telephone sets. But the business line still rings at home, which can be good or
13 bad. "Having it forwarded to the house makes it flexible because you don't have
14 to be at the office to answer the phone," Cindy said. "The drawback is you can't
15 ever get away from the phone. You sort of live your business all the time. It's
16 there at home with you."
17   This modern conflict of work and home affects many people. It's no longer
18 just business owners or professionals such as doctors who are at the beck and
19 call of their livelihood; even the average employee finds it difficult to get away
20 from work sometimes. Pagers, cell phones, and other devices can be a mixed

21 blessing, providing access and efficiency, yet at the same time, inconvenience and
22 interruption of family life and personal time.
23   This phenomenon has been explored extensively by Maggie Jackson, a
24 columnist and author of *What's Happening to Home: Balancing Work, Life and Refuge in the*
25 *Information Age.* The New York resident, who worked as a reporter for the *New*
26 *York Times* and the *Boston Globe,* said that technology is redefining home life and
27 blurring the boundaries between work and home. With the explosion of hi-tech
28 devices such as cell phones and PDAs, or personal digital assistants, she said,
29 "The march of technology into our lives is unstoppable."
30   While viewing technological development as a gift, Jackson warns that it
31 may require sacrifice as well. Mobile technology is turning homes into
32 workplaces, she said, citing the popularity of the computer armoire and a
33 modern sofa that make it easier to bring work into the living room. In coming
34 decades, she predicts that the lines between work and home will be even
35 dimmer, and people won't feel a need to hide their computers in fancy furniture.
36   Jackson reports that 70 percent of all employees must be accessible to their
37 jobs during off-hours and says that technology is chipping away at weekend and
38 vacation time. "It changes the parameters of a worker's private time," she said.
39 In addition, domestic life has moved from the home and neighborhood into the
40 workplace, she said, noting that employees may eat, socialize, and even work out
41 at the company. From work, parents may instant-message their children or
42 connect with latch-key kids via telephone or personal cell phone. Jackson says
43 that 60 million people bring their cell phones to work each day. Some children
44 even fax homework and report cards to Mom or Dad to check at the office.
45 "Home and work are becoming truly portable," Jackson said.
46   The sacrifices and costs of losing what have been boundaries between work
47 and home include a lack of refuge in the home and loss of private life. Jackson
48 advocates employer respect for the personal life of workers and commends
49 companies like Ernst & Young for making efforts to protect that privacy and
50 limit the on-call time of employees. Other drawbacks to the expansion of
51 technology include the loneliness and distance of virtual relationships, which
52 can give people the feeling of being together when they are actually apart.
53   "The proliferation of mobile technology is affecting the way we relate to
54 each other," said Jackson, who discussed parents who instant-message their
55 children to come down to dinner rather than shouting upstairs and those who
56 read bedtime books to children over the telephone while on a business trip. She
57 said that friends might use technology as a new form of togetherness by carrying
58 out their relationships via technology. "Face to face togetherness is the old
59 standard," she said. "Families are now portable, too." High-tech devices also
60 can invade the privacy of others when they interrupt performances, business
61 meetings, or dinner conversations, Jackson said.

So, what can be done about this technological invasion? Do we try to squelch it, live with it, or just find the right balance? We may find a clue in Jackson's depiction of a transition of the past. She said that when the Industrial Age gave way to the computer age, many people worried that the new devices would overtake their old way of life. And one wise observer summed their fears up when he warned people: "Be sure that we control these gadgets and not the other way around." That's not bad advice for today, either.

Fact-Finding Exercise

Read the passage again. Read the following statements. Check whether they are True (T) or False (F). If a statement is false, rewrite the statement so that it is true.

1. _____ T _____ F   Cindy has to be at her office in order to answer the business phone.

_____

2. _____ T _____ F   Only doctors and business owners must be accessible to their jobs at all times.

_____

3. _____ T _____ F   Maggie Jackson believes that we cannot stop technology in our lives.

_____

4. _____ T _____ F   Some people hide their computers in their living rooms.

_____

5. _____ T _____ F   Sixty million children fax their homework to their parents at work.

_____

6. _____ T _____ F   Modern technology has resulted in a loss of private life for some people.

_____

7. _____ T _____ F   Some companies try to protect the privacy of their workers.

_____

Reading Analysis

Read each question carefully. Circle the number or letter of the correct answer, or write your answer in the space provided.

1. What is the main idea of the passage?
    a. Modern technology has destroyed family life for many people.
    b. Sometimes work interferes with home life because of modern technology.
    c. Many people must be accessible to their jobs even when they are home.

2. Read line 3, **Take my sister Cindy.** This means
    a. Cindy is an example of a person who can't get away from work
    b. Cindy takes her high-tech gadgets to work
    c. Cindy is an example of a person who has a small business

3. a. Read lines 14–15. A **drawback** is
    1. an advantage
    2. a disadvantage
    3. a type of telephone

    b. In this sentence, what is an example of a drawback?

    _____

4. a. Read lines 17–22. **At the beck and call of their livelihood** means
    1. many people must telephone their employers every day
    2. many people have jobs that are very demanding
    3. many people cannot get away from their jobs when they are home

    b. A **mixed blessing** is
    1. an advantage
    2. a disadvantage
    3. an advantage and a disadvantage

5. Read lines 27–29. In this sentence, **the explosion** is

    a. a sudden increase in popularity
    b. the destruction of technology
    c. a personal digital assistant

6. Read lines 36–38. **Technology is chipping away at weekend and vacation time** means

    a. people have more free time because of modern technology
    b. people have less free time because of modern technology
    c. people have the same amount of free time because of modern technology

7. a. Read lines 39–41. **Domestic** life means

    1. professional life
    2. home and family life
    3. childhood life

    b. What are some examples of how domestic life has moved into the workplace?

    _____

8. a. Read lines 47–50. What is **Ernst & Young?**

    1. A job
    2. A company
    3. The authors of a book

    b. Jackson commends Ernst & Young for

    1. protecting the privacy of its employees
    2. developing the use of modern technology
    3. the loss of the private life of its employees

    c. **Commend** means

    1. dislike
    2. agree with
    3. praise

9. a. Read lines 53–56. The **proliferation** means the

    1. increase
    2. use
    3. drawback

b. What are two examples of how technology affects the way people relate to each other?

1. _____

2. _____

10. Read lines 62–63. **Squelch** means

a. enjoy
b. stop
c. continue

11. a. Read lines 66–68. **Not the other way around** means

1. be sure that the gadgets do not control us
2. be sure that we control the gadgets
3. be sure that we don't have too many gadgets

b. Another way to say **the other way around** is

1. backwards
2. vice versa
3. another direction

C. Word Forms

Part 1

In English, verbs change to nouns in several ways. Some verbs become nouns by adding the suffixes *-ion* or *-tion*, for example, *suggest (v.)*, *suggestion (n.)*. Complete each sentence with a correct form of the words on the left. **Use the simple past tense of the verb in either the affirmative or the negative form. Use the singular form of the nouns.**

expand *(v)*.
expansion *(n.)*

1. a. The Miller family recently _____ their home.

    b. They added two extra bedrooms and a bathroom to their home during the _____.

proliferate *(v.)*
proliferation *(n.)*

2. a. Last year, the use of cell phones greatly _____ among teenagers. Almost every teenager had one.

    b. This _____ helps working parents and their children keep in touch more easily.

depict *(v.)*
depiction *(n.)*

3. a. Vincent Van Gogh _____ sunflowers in one of his most famous paintings.

    b. In his _____, the bright, colorful flowers are in a beautiful vase on a table.

protect *(v.)*
protection *(n.)*

4. a. _____ from the sun is very important, especially at the beach.

    b. On her last vacation, Carla _____ her skin by using a very strong sunscreen lotion.

predict *(v.)*
prediction *(n.)*

5. a. The news reporter _____ a bright, sunny day yesterday. He said it would rain.

    b. However, his _____ was incorrect because it didn't rain at all.

Part 2

In English, the verb and noun forms of some words are the same, for example, *help (n.)* and *help (v.)*.

Complete each sentence with the correct form of the word on the left. **Use the correct tense of the verb in either the affirmative or the negative form. Use the singular or plural form of the noun. In addition, indicate whether you are using the noun *(n.)* or verb *(v.)* form.**

inconvenience

1. a. My sister _____ me when she came to pick me up
   (n., v.)
   an hour late.

   b. Because of this _____, I was late for my doctor's
   appointment.   *(n., v.)*

fear

2. a. When the computer age began, some people _____
   (n., v.)
   that modern technology would soon control our lives.

   b. However, these _____ lessened as people
   (n., v.)
   realized that computers can make our lives easier.

conduct

3. a. Maria never _____ business at home when she is
   (n., v.)
   with her family.

   b. This kind of _____ helps separate her personal life
   (n., v.)
   from her job.

change

4. a. Too many _____ are sometimes difficult for older
   (n., v.)
   people to make.

   b. Computers _____ my father's life. He still uses an
   (n., v.)
   old typewriter to write letters.

conflict

5. a. Some employees solve _____ between their home
   (n., v.)
   lives and their jobs by working fewer hours.

   b. But when Donna's job _____ with her home life, she
   (n., v.)
   needed to find a different job.

D. DICTIONARY SKILLS

Indicate the number of the definition for each word. Then write the synonym or meaning in the space provided. **Be sure to use the correct form of the verbs and nouns.**

1.

> **accessible** *adj* **1** able to be entered or reached: *The opera house is accessible by bus, subway, or car.* **2** easy to get to, *(syn.)* approachable: *He is an important man, but always accessible to his workers.*

Jackson reports that 70% of all employees must be (___)_____ to their jobs during off-hours and says that technology is chipping away at weekend and vacation time.

2.

> **boundary** *n* **1** a legal line dividing two places, *(syn.)* a border: *The boundary between the two towns (countries, cities) is shown by a line on the map.* **2** a limit of s.t.: *Some things are beyond the boundaries of human understanding.* **3** in sports, the limit of the court, field, etc.: *A ball must be within the boundary, not "out of bounds," to be played.*

Technology is redefining home life and blurring the (___)_____ between work and home.

3.

> **commend** *v* **1** to praise: *The teacher commended the students for doing well on the exam.* **2** to say that s.o. or s.t. is worthy and good to recommend. *She commended the hotel in her letter to me.* **3** to place in s.o. else's care. *I commended my child's health to the doctor and nurse.*

Jackson advocated employer respect for the personal life of workers and (___)_____ companies for making efforts to protect the privacy and limit the on-call time of employees.

4.

> **interrupt** *v* **1** to stop s.t. from continuing:
> *A bad storm interrupted telephone*
> *communications between the two islands.*
> **2** to start talking or doing s.t. in the middle
> of s.o.'s conversation or activity, to break in:
> *Our little boy always interrupts our*
> *conversations by asking questions.*

High-tech devices also can invade the privacy of others when they
(____)_____ performances, business meetings, or dinner
conversations.

Read the article a second time. Underline what you think are the main ideas. Then scan the article and fill in the following chart, using the sentences that you have underlined to help you. You will use this chart later to answer specific questions about the article.

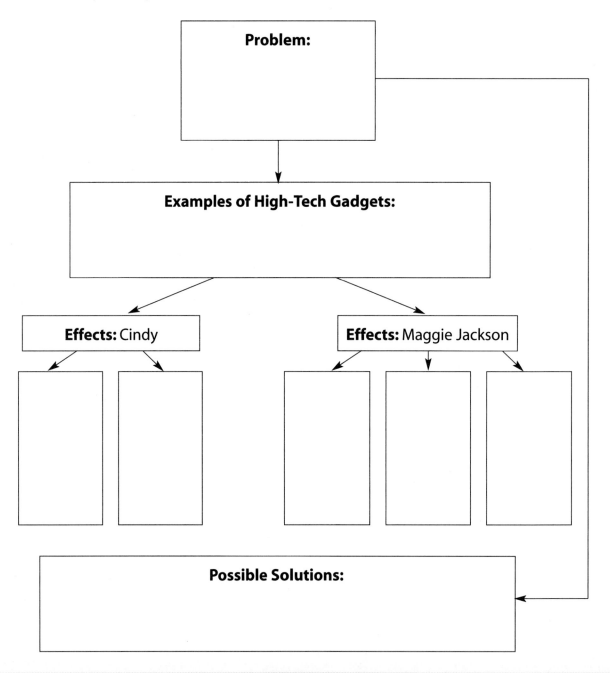

Problem:

Examples of High-Tech Gadgets:

Effects: Cindy

Effects: Maggie Jackson

Possible Solutions:

Information Organization Quiz and Summary

Read each question carefully. Use your notes and the chart on the previous page to answer the questions. Do not refer back to the text. Write your answers in the space provided under each question. When you are finished, write a brief summary of the article.

1. What problems can high-tech gadgets cause for some workers?

   _____

   _____

2. What types of high-tech gadgets can connect workers to their jobs even when they are not at work?

   _____

   _____

3. What are the positive effects of this technology?

   _____

   _____

4. What are the negative effects of this technology?

   _____

   _____

5. How can employers help to reduce the negative effects for their employees?

   _____

   _____

Summary

_____

_____

_____

_____

_____

_____

G. *Critical Thinking Strategies*

Read each question carefully. Write your response in the space provided. Remember that there is no one correct answer. Your response depends on what **you** think.

1. Maggie Jackson predicts that the lines between work and home will be even dimmer in coming decades, and people won't feel a need to hide their computers in fancy furniture. What is Ms. Jackson inferring about people today?

    _____

    _____

2. Jackson says, "The proliferation of mobile technology is affecting the way we relate to each other." What kinds of relationships is she talking about? How are those relationships changing?

    _____

    _____

3. What do you think is Cindy's opinion about the effects of modern technology on her family's life? Why do you think this?

    _____

    _____

4. What do you think is Maggie Jackson's opinion about the effects of high-tech gadgets on family life? Why do you think this?

    _____

    _____

H. *Follow-up Discussion* AND *Writing Activities*

1. Modern technology enables workers to connect with their jobs at all times. Work with a partner. Make a list of both the advantages and disadvantages of this phenomenon.

2. Make a list of all the technological gadgets you have. How much time do you spend each day using these gadgets? Compare your estimates with your classmates'. Discuss what you would do if you no longer had each one of these gadgets. How would your life change? How would your relationships with other people change?

3. Use the list of technological gadgets you created in #3. As a class, decide which gadget is the most essential one and which gadget is the least essential one. What are your reasons for your choices?

4. **Write in your journal.** Do you think modern technology has an effect on your personal relationships? How? Give examples of its effects.

Cloze Quiz

Chapter 2: Close to Home

Read the passage on this page. Fill in the blanks below with one word from the list. Use each word once.

access	boundaries	connect	interruption	technology
addition	companies	devices	phenomenon	unstoppable
advocates	conduct	employees	protect	vacation
affects	conflict	homework	take	workplace

Some people can never get away from work these days. _____ (1) my sister Cindy. Cindy recalls attending her kids' soccer games with an oversized walkie-talkie in hand so she could _____ (2) business, if necessary. This modern _____ (3) of work and home _____ (4) many people. Pagers, cell phones, and other _____ (5) can be a mixed blessing, providing _____ (6) and efficiency, yet at the same time, inconvenience and _____ (7) of family life and personal time.

This _____ (8) has been explored extensively by Maggie Jackson. This reporter said that _____ (9) is redefining home life and blurring the _____ (10) between work and home. "The march of technology into our lives is _____ (11)."

Jackson reports that 70 percent of all _____ (12) must be accessible to their jobs during off-hours, including weekends and _____ (13) time. In _____ (14), domestic life has moved from the home and neighborhood into the _____ (15), she said. From work, parents may instant-message their children or _____ with (16) latch-key kids via cell phone. Some children even fax _____ and (17) report cards to Mom or Dad to check at the office.

Jackson _____ employer respect for the personal life of (18) workers and commends _____ like Ernst & Young for making (19) efforts to _____ that privacy. (20)

The Birth-Order Myth
by Alfie Kohn
Health

Prereading Preparation

1. How many brothers and sisters do you have? Are you the youngest? Are you the oldest?

2. Many people believe that birth order affects an individual's personality or intelligence. What do you think about this idea?

3. a. Write some general statements describing your classmates' personalities.

   b. Make a chart on the blackboard of how many people in the class are only children, firstborn, secondborn, thirdborn, etc.

   c. Form groups according to birth order; in other words, all the only children will form one group, all the firstborns will form one group, etc. In your groups, describe your personalities. Make a list of the personality characteristics that are common to all of you.

   d. Write the information for each group on the blackboard. Compare all the groups' responses. Discuss how these responses correspond to the descriptions of the other students in the class.

1 "No wonder he's so charming and funny—he's the baby of the family!" "She
2 works hard trying to please the boss. I bet she's a firstborn." "Anyone that
3 selfish has to be an only child."

4 It's long been part of folk wisdom that birth order strongly affects
5 personality, intelligence, and achievement. However, most of the research
6 claiming that firstborns are radically different from other children has been
7 discredited, and it now seems that any effects of birth order on intelligence or
8 personality will likely be washed out by all the other influences in a person's life.
9 In fact, the belief in the permanent impact of birth order, according to Toni
10 Falbo, a social psychologist at the University of Texas at Austin, "comes from the
11 psychological theory that your personality is fixed by the time you're six. That
12 assumption simply is incorrect."

13 The better, later, and larger studies are less likely to find birth order a
14 useful predictor of anything. When two Swiss social scientists, Cecile Ernst and
15 Jules Angst, reviewed 1,500 studies a few years ago, they concluded that "birth-
16 order differences in personality . . . are nonexistent in our sample. In
17 particular, there is no evidence for a 'firstborn personality.'"

Putting Birth Order in Context

18 Of the early studies that seemed to show birth order mattered, most failed
19 to recognize how other factors could confuse the issue. Take family size: Plenty
20 of surveys showed that eldest children were overrepresented among high
21 achievers. However, that really says less about being a firstborn than about not
22 having many siblings, or any at all. After all, any group of firstborns is going to
23 include a disproportionate number of children from small families, since every
24 family has a firstborn but fewer have a fourthborn. Most experts now believe
25 that position in the family means little when taken out of the context of
26 *everything* going on in a particular household–whether sibling rivalry is promoted
27 or discouraged, for instance.

28 Parents who believe that firstborns are more capable or deserving may treat
29 them differently, thus setting up a self-fulfilling prophecy.

Old Theories Die Hard

30 Consider the question of whether birth order affects achievement or
31 intelligence. Many experts today suggest that birth order plays no role at all.
32 When Judith Blake, a demographer at the University of California, Los Angeles,

looked at birth patterns before 1938 and compared them to SAT[1] scores for that group of children, she found no connection. On the other hand, the *number* of siblings does matter. "Small families are, on average, much more supportive of the kind of verbal ability that helps people succeed in school," Blake says. The reason, she believes, is that parental attention is diluted in larger families.

As for effects on personality, results are mixed. Research suggests that you're somewhat more likely to be outgoing, well-adjusted and independent if you grew up with few or no siblings. Two recent studies, however, found no differences on the basis of size alone. The only certainty is that there don't seem to be any *disadvantages* to growing up in a small family—including being an only child. After reviewing 141 studies, Falbo and a colleague found that being raised with or without siblings doesn't affect personality in predictable ways. Where small differences were found—such as in achievement motivation—they favored the only children.

Do Kids Need More Space?

If position doesn't control destiny and family size has only a minor impact, what about spacing between children? Although little research has been conducted, some psychologists believe there are more advantages to having kids far apart rather than close together. Some specialists caution that siblings close in age may be treated as a single unit.

This is eyebrow-raising news, given that parents are sometimes advised not to wait too long before having a second child. However, different studies have led to different conclusions. One found that a firstborn was more likely to have high self-esteem if his or her sibling was *less* than two years younger. Another indicated that spacing had no impact on social competence, and others note positive effects for boys but not for girls.

As with birth order, cautions about jumping to conclusions may be ignored by the general public. As Blake says: "You're never going to completely put to rest what people think is fun to believe."

---

[1]The Scholastic Aptitude Test; the scores on this test are used to determine high school students' ability to do college work.

Fact-Finding Exercise

Read the passage once. Then read the following statements. Scan the article quickly to find out if each statement is true (T) or false (F). If a statement is false, change it so that it is true.

1. ____ T ____ F   The firstborn child in the family is different from the other children in the family.

_____

2. ____ T ____ F   Studies will probably find that birth order affects personality.

_____

3. ____ T ____ F   The number of children in a family affects personality more than birth order does.

_____

4. ____ T ____ F   Growing up in a small family has many disadvantages.

_____

5. ____ T ____ F   Many experts believe that birth order does not affect intelligence.

_____

6. ____ T ____ F   Some people believe it is better for a family to have children far apart rather than close in age.

_____

Reading Analysis

Read each question carefully. Circle the number or letter of the correct answer, or write your answer in the space provided.

1. Read line 1.

   a. What follows the dash (—)?

      1. The reason he's charming and funny
      2. Extra information about him
      3. Information about his family

   b. **He's the baby of the family** means

      1. he's very young
      2. he's the youngest child
      3. he's very immature

2. Read the first paragraph. These statements are examples of

   a. the author's beliefs
   b. birth-order myths
   c. facts about birth order

3. In lines 5–8, **discredited** means

   a. proved correct
   b. misunderstood
   c. found to be wrong

4. Read lines 5–12.

   a. This statement means that, as a result of other influences, the effects of birth order

      1. will disappear
      2. will become clean
      3. will combine

   b. What information follows **in fact?**

      1. True information about birth order
      2. Information about Toni Falbo
      3. Information to support the previous idea

    c. What word in these sentences is a synonym for **assumption?**

       1. influence
       2. belief
       3. fact

5. Read lines 14–17.

    a. What do the dots between **personality** and **are** indicate?

       1. Some words have been deleted.
       2. Both Ernst and Angst are speaking at the same time.
       3. It is a quotation.

    b. What does **in particular** mean?

       1. Part of
       2. Specifically
       3. In addition

6. In line 19, what does **take** mean?

_____

7. Read lines 24–27.

    a. Why is ***everything*** in italics?

_____

    b. The author means that

       1. sibling rivalry is important
       2. position in the family is important
       3. all things that are going on are important

    c. What is the purpose of the dash (—) after **household?**

       1. To add extra information
       2. To give an example
       3. To give a definition

    d. How do you know this is the purpose of the dash?

_____

8. Read lines 32–35.

    a. What is the **SAT?**

_____

b. How do you know?

_____

c. This type of information is called
   1. an abbreviation
   2. a footnote
   3. an asterisk

d. **On the other hand** indicates
   1. more information
   2. an example
   3. an opposing idea

e. Why is *number* in italics?

_____

9. Read lines 38–43. **Results are mixed** means
   a. different people got different results
   b. everyone got the same results
   c. different people were confused about their results

10. Read lines 47–51. **Spacing between children** means
    a. how far apart children stand
    b. how far apart children are in age
    c. how far apart children are from their parents

11. Read lines 52–53. **Eyebrow-raising news** is
    a. wonderful
    b. terrible
    c. surprising

Part 1

In English, verbs can change to nouns in several ways. Some verbs become nouns by adding the suffix -ment, for example, improve (v.), improvement (n.). Complete each sentence with the correct form of the words on the left. **Use the correct tense of the verbs, in either the affirmative or the negative form. Use the singular or plural form of the nouns.**

encourage (v.)
encouragement (n.)

1. a. When Kevin gets married and has children, he _____ them to work hard.

    b. Kevin believes that strong parental _____ makes children successful.

achieve (v.)
achievement (n.)

2. a. Most big _____ result from hard work.

    b. We may not always be successful, but surely we _____ anything if we don't try.

improve (v.)
improvement (n.)

3. a. The mayor plans to make significant _____ to all the city parks.

    b. First, the mayor _____ the tennis courts and baseball fields. Then, she will put in new park benches.

state (v.)
statement (n.)

4. a. This morning the president _____ that he would not run for reelection.

    b. He made this surprising _____ at a news conference in Washington, D.C.

treat (v.)
treatment (n.)

5. a. Doctors usually _____ infections with antibiotics such as penicillin.

    b. A severe infection may require several _____ over a long period of time.

Part 2

In English, some adjectives become nouns by deleting a final -t and adding -ce, for example, *important (adj.), importance (n.).*

Complete each sentence with the correct form of the words on the left.

competent *(adj.)*
competence *(n.)*

1. a. Winifred is an extremely _____ businesswoman.
    b. After working at a firm for only a few years, she developed enough _____ to start her own business, which has become very successful.

intelligent *(adj.)*
intelligence *(n.)*

2. a. It is impossible to measure _____ on a test because people have different kinds of aptitudes.
    b. Besides, even a very _____ person can become nervous and do poorly on a test.

permanent *(adj.)*
permanence *(n.)*

3. a. Peter has never had a really _____ home.
    b. Peter's parents have always moved from one city to another every few years, so the idea of _____ is something very strange to him.

significant *(adj.)*
significance *(n.)*

4. a. There has been a _____ decrease in the population of this city in the last ten years.
    b. The _____ of this population decline in schools is that there tend to be fewer students in each class.

different *(adj.)*
difference *(n.)*

5. a. I can't taste any _____ between regular coffee and decaffeinated coffee.
    b. However, I drink them at _____ times of the day. For instance, I drink regular coffee in the morning, but I drink decaffeinated coffee in the evening.

D. DICTIONARY SKILLS

Indicate the number of the definition for each word. Then write the synonym or meaning in the space provided. **Be sure to use the correct forms of the verbs and nouns.**

1.
> **radical** *adj* **1** of or from the root; fundamental: *~ changes.* **2** *(esp politics)* favoring complete and drastic changes.

People no longer believe that there is a (____)_____ difference between firstborn children and other children.

2.
> **claim** *v* **1** demand recognition of the fact that one is, or owns, or has a right to (something): *He ~ed to be the owner of/~ed that he owned the land.* **2** say that something is a fact: *He ~ed to be the best tennis player in the school.* **3** (of things) need; deserve: *There are several matters that ~ my attention.*

People no longer (____)_____ that there is a radical difference between firstborn children and other children.

3.
> **fix** *v* **1** make firm or fast; fasten (something) so that it cannot be moved: *~ shelves to a wall.* **2** (of objects) attract and hold (the attention): *This unusual sight kept his attention ~ed.* **3** set; determine or decide: *~ the rent/a date for a meeting; ~ed the blame.* **4** mend; repair: *They've ~ed all the broken windows.* **5** put in order; prepare: *~ one's hair,* brush and comb it.

The assumption that heredity and our environment (____)_____ our personality by the time we're six is incorrect.

4.
> **promote** *v* **1** give (a person) higher position or rank: *He was ~ed sergeant/to the rank of sergeant.* **2** help to organize and start; help the progress of: *try to ~ good feelings (between . . .).*

Some parents (____)_____ sibling rivalry among their children.

Information Organization

Read the article a second time. Underline what you think are the main ideas. Then scan the article and complete the following outline, using the sentences that you have underlined to help you. You will use this outline later to answer specific questions about the article.

I. The Myth and the Reality About Birth Order
    A. The Myth:
    B. The Reality:

II.
    A. The findings of Cecile Ernst and Jules Angst
        1. Birth-order differences in personality are nonexistent
        2.
    B.
        1. Birth order does not affect intelligence; she looked at birth patterns before 1938 and compared them to SAT scores for that group of children, and she found no connection

III.
    A.
        1. It does affect intelligence; small families tend to be more supportive of the kind of verbal ability that helps people succeed in school
    B.
        1. Parents who believe that firstborns are more capable or deserving may treat them differently, thus setting up a self-fulfilling prophecy
    C.
        1. Some psychologists believe there are more advantages to having kids far apart
        2. One study found that a firstborn was more likely to have high self-esteem if his or her sibling was *less* than two years younger

IV.
    A. You're more likely to be outgoing, well adjusted, and independent if you grew up with few or no siblings
    B.
    C. One study indicated that spacing had no impact on social competence

Read each question carefully. Use your notes to answer the questions. Do not refer back to the text. Write your answers in the space provided under each question. When you are finished, write a brief summary of the article.

1. a. What do many people believe about birth order?

    _____

    _____

    b. What is the truth about birth order?

    _____

    _____

2. What were the research results about birth order?

    _____

    _____

3. What are three family factors that may have more effect on personality and intelligence than birth order? Explain each one.

    a. _____

    _____

    _____

    b. _____

    _____

    _____

    c. _____

    _____

    _____

4. Were all the results of research about family size and birth order the same?

_____

_____

Summary

_____

_____

_____

_____

_____

_____

G. *Critical Thinking Strategies*

Read each question carefully. Write your response in the space provided. Remember that there is no one correct answer. Your response depends on what **you** think.

1. The author writes, "Parents who believe that firstborns are more capable or deserving may treat them differently, thus setting up a self-fulfilling prophecy." The self-fulfilling prophecy is that children live up to their parents' expectations. How do you think parents influence their children by treating them differently?

   _____

   _____

   _____

   _____

2. According to the article, the number of siblings a person has affects his or her personality. As Judith Blake says, "Small families are, on average, much more supportive of the kind of verbal ability that helps people succeed in school." The reason, she believes, is that parental attention is diluted in larger families. Why do you think parental attention might be diluted in larger families? Do you agree with this theory? Explain your answer.

   _____

   _____

   _____

   _____

3. One study found that a firstborn was more likely to have high self-esteem if his or her sibling was *less* than two years younger. Another indicated that spacing had no impact on social competence, and others note positive effects for boys but not for girls. What conclusion can you make about these different studies?

   _____

   _____

   _____

   _____

4. The studies that the author refers to in this article came up with very different results. How do you think we might explain these different findings?

_____

_____

_____

_____

5. Read the last paragraph of the article. What does Judith Blake mean? Why may people ignore the findings about the birth-order myth?

_____

_____

_____

_____

6. What do you think the author's opinion about birth order is? Why do you think so?

_____

_____

_____

_____

H. *Follow-up Discussion* AND *Writing Activities*

1. What stereotypes do you have in your country about children and birth order? How do you think these myths came about?

2. a. Refer to the Birth Order Survey on page 55. As a class, add more pairs of adjectives to complete the survey.

   b. After you have finished the questionnaire, go outside your class alone or in pairs. Survey two or three people. Then bring back your data and combine it with the other students' information. How do your results compare with the results you obtained in your class? Do you think the idea of birth-order characteristics is convincing, or is it a myth?

3. Think about your in-class and questionnaire findings and the article you have just read.
   a. What was your opinion about birth-order myths before you did your surveys and read this article? Do you still have that opinion?
   b. Does the information you collected support the author's findings or conflict with them? Give reasons for your answer.

4. **Write in your journal.** What do you think are the advantages and disadvantages of being an only child? Explain your opinion. Indicate if you are an only child or whether or not you would like to be an only child.

BIRTH-ORDER SURVEY

The purpose of this questionnaire is to collect data regarding birth order. Please answer the following questions.

1. Do you have siblings? How many?

   _____

2. What is your order of birth? That is, are you an only child, firstborn, secondborn, thirdborn? *Are you also the youngest child?*

   _____

3. Please indicate one of each of the pairs of adjectives that describes your personality.

1. anxious/confident	13. mature/immature
2. patient/impatient	14. funny/serious
3. boring/interesting	15.
4 talkative/quiet	16.
5. understanding/insensitive	17.
6. diligent/lazy	18.
7. friendly/disagreeable	19.
8. competitive/cooperative	20.
9. considerate/thoughtless	21.
10. creative/unimaginative	22.
11. curious/indifferent	23.
12. dependent/independent	24.

Cloze Quiz

Chapter 3: The Birth-Order Myth

Read the passage on this page. Fill in the blanks below with one word from the list. Use each word once.

affects	differences	evidence	permanent	scientists
assumption	different	however	personality	studies
birth	discredited	influences	predictor	theory
concluded	effects	intelligence	research	time

It's long been part of folk wisdom that birth order strongly

_____ personality, _____, and achievement.
    (1)   (2)

_____, most of the _____ claiming that firstborns
    (3)   (4)

are radically _____ from other children has been
             (5)

_____, and it now seems that any _____ of birth
    (6)   (7)

order on intelligence or _____ will likely be washed out by all
                   (8)

the other _____ in a person's life. In fact, the belief in the
          (9)

_____ impact of _____ order, according to Toni
    (10)   (11)

Falbo, "comes with the psychological _____ that your
                           (12)

personality is fixed by the _____ you're six. That
                  (13)

_____ simply is incorrect."
    (14)

The better, later, and larger _____ are less likely to find birth
                 (15)

order a useful _____ of anything. When two Swiss social
        (16)

_____, Cecile Ernst and Jules Angst, reviewed 1,500 studies a few
    (17)

years ago, they _____ that "birth-order _____ in
           (18)   (19)

personality . . . are nonexistent in our sample. In particular, there is no

_____ for a 'firstborn personality.'"
    (20)

Unit 1 Review

J. Crossword Puzzle

Read the clues on the next page. Write the answers in the correct spaces in the puzzle.

Crossword Clues

Across

1. The opposite of **no**
7. Our children are our _____.
10. I _____ a car. I'll drive you to work.
13. A clue
15. A supposition or belief
16. Stop; suppress
17. Feelings, such as happiness, anger, or joy
18. This, _____, these, those
20. Gadgets
22. Back up

Down

2. Worker
3. The past tense of **is**
4. Mostly
5. The past tense of **run**
6. When we praise someone, we _____ her.
8. A great increase or widespread use
9. Disadvantage
11. Competition between people
12. Surroundings; everything around you
14. You look like your mother. You _____ your mother.
19. The past tense of **hit**
21. The opposite of **down**

1. The articles in Unit 1 all relate to what influences our satisfaction. Discuss what factors in our lives we can control or change, e.g., jobs and happiness, and those we cannot, e.g., birth order. Which factors do you think are the most important towards achieving satisfaction? Why? Explain your reasons.

2. How can modern technology affect our happiness? Do new high-tech gadgets help us feel happier, or do they sometimes have a different effect? Discuss your answers with your class.

3. Do you think modern technology brings families closer together, or farther apart? Why? Give some examples of specific types of technology and how they may affect family life.

1. The video is about wireless computers that people can use anywhere to access the Internet. What are some advantages and disadvantages of this kind of technology?

2. Read the questions and watch the video. Answer the questions in groups and then discuss them with the whole class.

   a. What is a "hot spot"? What kind of technology is used at hot spots to connect people to the Internet? Do users need to buy any extra equipment for their computers in order to use hot spots?

   b. One man calls the hot spot he uses an "outdoor office." Do you believe the ability to conduct business outdoors—for example, at lunchtime or on weekends—is an advantage or a mixed blessing? Why?

   c. A woman in the video who usually works at home enjoys going to a hot spot to work. What advantages does it have for her? Does it have any disadvantages?

   d. Will the use of wireless technology contribute to blurring the boundaries between work and home? Why or why not?

   e. Do you think most people go to hot spots for business or pleasure? Do you think students would go to hot spots to do school work or send email?

3. Right now, no company offers nationwide coverage for computers equipped with wireless capability. What are your predictions for the future of wireless technology? Will it expand nationwide? Would you and people you know use hot spots if they could? Is there a hot spot in your community?

INFOTRAC® Research Activity
COLLEGE EDITION
The Online Library

There are many types of lightweight portable computers, also called notebook computers, and the market for them is expanding. Search InfoTrac by typing in these words: "notebook computers; newspapers" and "notebook computers; evaluation." Limit your search to the last year or two. Read the *titles* of the articles, and scan a few articles to find information that you are interested in, such as the types of Internet access various computers offer, the price, the weight, and special features offered by these high-tech gadgets. Take notes on the articles and make a chart comparing computers. Report your findings to the group or whole class.

UNIT 2

SAFETY AND HEALTH

Why So Many More Americans Die in Fires

by Donald G. McNeil, Jr.

The New York Times

Prereading Preparation

1. What are some ways that fires start?

2. What are some things that we can do to prevent fires?

3. Are there many fires in your city?

4. If someone has a fire in his or her home in your country, how will the neighbors react?

5. If someone has a fire in his or her home in the United States, how do you think the neighbors will react?

6. Do you think all fires are accidental?

7. Look at the title. What do you think this article will be about?

1   In some ways, the United States has made spectacular progress. Fires no
2   longer destroy 18,000 buildings as they did in the Great Chicago Fire of 1871, or
3   kill half a town of 2,400 people, as they did the same night in Peshtigo,
4   Wisconsin. Other than the Beverly Hills Supper Club fire in Kentucky in 1977, it
5   has been four decades since more than 100 Americans died in a fire.

6   But even with such successes, the United States still has one of the worst
7   fire death rates in the world—worse than all of western Europe and Asia. Safety
8   experts say the problem is neither money nor technology, but the indifference of
9   a country that just will not take fires seriously enough.

10 American fire departments are some of the world's fastest and best-
11 equipped. They have to be. The United States has twice Japan's population and
12 40 times as many fires. It spends far less on preventing fires than on fighting
13 them. And American fire-safety lessons are aimed almost entirely at children,
14 who die in disproportionately large numbers in fires but who, contrary to
15 popular myth, start very few of them.

16 Experts say the fatal error is an attitude that fires are not really anyone's
17 fault. That is not so in other countries, where both public education and the law
18 treat fires as either a personal failing or a crime. Japan has many wood houses; of
19 the estimated 48 fires in world history that burned more than 10,000 buildings,
20 Japan has had 27. Penalties for causing a severe fire by negligence can be as high
21 as life imprisonment. Have a simple house fire, and "your neighbors may ask you
22 to move away," said Philip Schaenman, a fire-safety consultant, whose Tridata
23 Corporation of Arlington, Va., analyzes other countries' fire-safety programs.
24 Officials with loudspeakers address crowds at fires, embarrassing those
25 responsible and preaching fire safety.

26 Most European countries have tougher building codes and insurance laws.
27 In the Netherlands, every room must have two exits. In France, to deter
28 landlord arson, insurers are not allowed to repay the full cost of damage. In
29 Switzerland, they pay only if an identical structure is rebuilt.

30 Public education is also better in Asia and Europe. Korea holds
31 neighborhood fire drills. Hong Kong apartment buildings have fire marshals.
32 The Japanese learn to use extinguishers at work. In England, the London Fire
33 Brigade spends roughly $1 million a year on fire-safety commercials.

34 In the United States, most education dollars are spent in elementary
35 schools. But the lessons are aimed at too limited an audience; just 9 percent of
36 all fire deaths are caused by children playing with matches.

37 Adults are the ones who leave the pans on the stove, smoke in bed, overload
38 house wiring, and buy unsafe heaters. Adults fail to buy fire extinguishers,

39 remove smoke-detector batteries, and do dangerous things like throw water into
40 pots of flaming French fries.
41   The United States continues to rely more on technology than laws or social
42 pressure. There are smoke detectors in 85 percent of all homes. Some local
43 building codes now require home sprinklers. New heaters and irons shut
44 themselves off if they are tipped. Eventually, new stoves will turn themselves off
45 if left on too long.
46   A handful of towns are fining people who have serious fires because they let
47 smoke detectors go dead, said John Ottoson, a senior analyst with the U.S. Fire
48 Administration. He knew of one landlord who was charged with manslaughter
49 when tenants were killed. But without more such changes in perception, the
50 United States seems unlikely to close the gap between the rate of fire fatalities in
51 the United States and other countries.

Fact-Finding Exercise

Read the passage once. Then read the following statements. Scan the article quickly to find out if each statement is true (T) or false (F). If a statement is false, change it so that it is true.

1. ____ T ____ F   The fire death rate in the United States is worse than those of Western Europe and Asia.

_____

2. ____ T ____ F   The United States has more fires than Japan.

_____

3. ____ T ____ F   Children start most of the fires that occur in the United States.

_____

4. ____ T ____ F   Japan has had more than half of the fires in world history that burned more than 10,000 buildings.

_____

5. ____ T ____ F   In France, insurers are not allowed to repay the full cost of fire damage.

_____

6. ____ T ____ F   Most homes in the United States do not have smoke detectors.

_____

7. ____ T ____ F   The high fire death rate in the United States is the result of bad technology.

_____

Read each question carefully. Circle the number or letter of the correct answer, or write your answer in the space provided.

1. In line 2 and in line 3, what does **they** refer to?
   a. People
   b. Buildings
   c. Fires

2. a. In line 3, what is **Peshtigo?**

   _____

   b. In line 4, what is **Wisconsin?**

   _____

3. In line 5, how much time is four decades?
   a. 4 years
   b. 40 years
   c. 400 years

4. Read lines 4–5. How many people died in the Beverly Hills Supper Club fire?
   a. More than 100 people
   b. Fewer than 100 people

5. a. Read lines 10–12. What does **they have to be** mean?

   _____

   _____

   b. What is the purpose of this sentence?
      1. Explanation
      2. Emphasis
      3. Contrast

6. Read lines 16–18. What does **That is not so in other countries** mean?

   _____

   _____

7. Read lines 27–28.

    a. What does **deter** mean?

        1. Punish

        2. Cause

        3. Prevent

    b. What does **arson** mean?

        1. To start a fire accidentally

        2. To start a fire deliberately

    c. What is a **landlord?**

        1. A person who owns a building

        2. A person who rents a place to live

8. In line 44, what does **eventually** refer to?

    a. Right now

    b. In the future

    c. Recently

9. Read lines 46–48.

    a. What does **handful** mean?

        1. A large number

        2. A small number

    b. **Fining** people means

        1. putting people in jail

        2. making people leave town

        3. charging people money

10. Read lines 48–49.

    a. What are **tenants?**

        1. People who rent apartments

        2. People who own apartments

        3. People who start fires

    b. What happened to the tenants?

        1. They went to jail.

        2. They moved.

        3. They died.

    c. What does **manslaughter** mean?

1. Robbery
2. Arson
3. Murder

11. Read lines 49–51.

    a. **The United States seems unlikely to close the gap** means

1. the United States will probably close the gap
2. the United States probably won't close the gap

    b. A **gap** is a

1. space
2. number
3. difference

    c. What does **fatalities** mean?

1. Deaths
2. Injuries
3. Damages

C. Word Forms

Part 1

In English, some adjectives become nouns by deleting the final -t and adding -ce, for example, *independent (adj.), independence (n.)*

Complete each sentence with the correct form of the words on the left.

important *(adj.)*
importance *(n.)*

1. a. It is extremely _____ to keep fresh batteries in your smoke detector.
    b. I cannot overemphasize the vital _____ of this practice—it could save your life one day.

negligent *(adj.)*
negligence *(n.)*

2. a. Mr. and Mrs. O'Hara were accused of criminal _____ when their house caught fire while their children were home alone.
    b. They had also been quite _____ about keeping matches away from their children; in fact, that's how the fire started.

dependent *(adj.)*
dependence *(n.)*

3. a. Most city people have more _____ on public transportation than they do on cars.
    b. They tend to be so _____ on trains and buses because street traffic is usually very heavy.

indifferent *(adj.)*
indifference *(n.)*

4. a. Chris shows such _____ to his classes that I'm afraid he's going to fail them.
    b. He's not only _____ to his courses; he doesn't care about his job, either.

excellent *(adj.)*
excellence *(n.)*

5. a. This particular model of car is an _____ automobile.
    b. In fact, it has won an award for _____ three years in a row.

Part 2

In English, some adjectives become nouns by adding the suffix *-ity,* for example, *equal (adj.), equality (n.).*

Complete each sentence with the correct form of the words on the left. **Use the singular or plural form of the nouns.**

fatal *(adj.)*
fatality *(n.)*

1. a. Yesterday, Tony saw a _____ accident on the highway.
    b. A car collided with a truck; there were several _____.

public *(adj.)*
publicity *(n.)*

2. a. Most film actors enjoy being in the _____ eye.
    b. In other words, they like getting a lot of _____ from the press.

safe *(adj.)*
safety *(n.)*

3. a. Many jobs that are considered _____ today used to be very dangerous.
    b. The reason these jobs are less hazardous now is because laws have been passed to ensure the reasonable _____ of employees.

responsible *(adj.)*
responsibility *(n.)*

4. a. Parents have serious _____ toward their children.
    b. For instance, parents are unquestionably _____ for their children's safety, health, education, and socialization.

possible *(adj.)*
possibility *(n.)*

5. a. When we worked on the math problem, we realized that there were several _____ solutions.
    b. Of all the _____, however, we chose the simplest explanation because it was the clearest.

D. DICTIONARY SKILLS

Choose the appropriate definition for each word. Then write the number and synonym or meaning in the space provided. **Be sure to use the correct form of the verbs and nouns.**

1.
> **negligence** *n* **1** carelessness; failure to take proper care or precautions: *The accident was due to ~.* **2** a negligent act.

Penalties for causing a severe fire by (____)_____ can be as high as life imprisonment.

2.
> **address** *v* **1** make a speech to: *Mr. Green will now ~ the meeting.* **2** speak to, using a title: *Don't ~ me as "Colonel"; I'm only a major.* **3** write the name and address on a letter, etc.

Officials with loudspeakers (____)_____ crowds at fires, preaching fire safety.

3.
> **marshal** *n* **1** officer of the highest rank in the military forces of some countries. **2** official in charge of important public events or ceremonies: *grand ~ of the parade.* **3** federal official with functions similar to those of a sheriff. **4** head of a fire or police department in some U.S. cities.

Hong Kong apartment buildings have fire (____)_____ who help people get out of a burning building safely.

4.
> **pressure** *n* **1** pressing. **2** (amount of) force exerted on or against something: *air ~.* **3** force or influence: *The union put ~ on him to vote for the bill,* **4** something that is difficult to bear: *the ~ of taxation.*

The United States continues to rely more on technology than on laws or social (____)_____.

Read the article a second time. Underline what you think are the main ideas. Then scan the article and complete the following table, using the sentences that you have underlined to help you. You will use this table later to answer specific questions about the article. Not all the boxes will be filled in.

	The United States	**Europe**	**Asia**
People's attitudes toward fires	1. People:	1. Public education and the law:	1. Public education and the law:
How countries deal with fires	1. American fire departments: 2.	1. In the Netherlands: 2. In France: 3. In Switzerland:	In Japan: 1. 2. 3.
Public education	1. Fire-safety lessons:	1. In England:	1. Korea: 2. Hong Kong: 3. Japan:
Technology for fire prevention	1. 2. 3. 4.		
How attitudes towards fires are changing	1. 2.		

Information Organization Quiz and Summary

Read each question carefully. Use your notes to answer the questions. Do not refer back to the text. Write your answers in the space provided under each question. When you are finished, write a brief summary of the article.

1. What is the difference in attitudes toward fires between Americans and people in other countries?

   _____

   _____

   _____

2. In general, what is the difference between how fires are dealt with in Asia and in Western Europe and how they are dealt with in the United States?

   _____

   _____

   _____

3. Is public education about fire safety different in the United States from public education in Asia and Europe? Why, or why not?

   _____

   _____

   _____

4. How are Americans' attitudes toward fire changing?

   _____

   _____

   _____

Summary

_____

_____

_____

_____

_____

G. *Critical Thinking Strategies*

Read each question carefully. Write your response in the space provided. Remember that there is no one correct answer. Your response depends on what **you** think.

1. Read the first paragraph. How does the author feel that the United States has made progress?

   _____

   _____

   _____

   _____

2. In lines 11 and 12, the author states, "The United States has twice Japan's population, and 40 times as many fires." What do you think this information implies?

   _____

   _____

   _____

   _____

3. Read lines 12–15.

   a. What does the author think of the United States' fire-prevention methods?

   _____

   _____

   _____

   _____

   b. What does the author think the United States should do to lower its fire death rate?

   _____

   _____

   _____

   _____

4. Read lines 18–23. According to this article, if you had a house fire in Japan, why might your neighbors ask you to move away?

_____

_____

_____

_____

5. Read lines 27–29. What do insurers think some landlords might do to their property? Why do you think they might do this?

_____

_____

_____

_____

6. Read lines 46–49. How do you think these two examples show a change in Americans' attitudes toward fires?

_____

_____

_____

_____

H. *Follow-up Discussion* AND *Writing Activities*

1. a. Read the following list of fires. Which fires were caused by negligence?

   1. Harry fell asleep while he was smoking in bed, and his house burned down.
   2. Lightning struck a house, which burned to the ground.
   3. Regina was frying chicken. When the fat caught fire, she tried to put the fire out with water, and the fire spread to the entire kitchen.
   4. The wind blew down an electrical power line and set fire to a store.

   b. Think about the fires that were caused by negligence. How could these fires have been prevented?

2. Work in pairs or small groups. The owners of an apartment building have asked you to make a list of building codes for the new building they are planning to construct.

3. Work in pairs or small groups. You are on a committee whose job is to create tougher fire laws for your city. Write two new laws and explain your reasons for each.

4. Work with a partner. Make a list of things you should not do that could cause a fire at home.

5. Work with a partner. Make a list of things you can do at home to prevent a fire.

6. **Write in your journal.** What are people's attitudes toward fires in your country? How are these attitudes similar to those in the United States? How are they different? Express your ideas about this.

Surfing THE *INTERNET*

Use the Internet to find out about the worst fire in history. Where was it? When did it occur? How much damage did it cause? How many people were killed?

Optional Activity: Use the Internet to learn about the worst fire in your country or area of the world. When did it take place? Where did it occur? How many people were killed? How much damage did it cause? Report your findings to the class. Compare the fires you researched.

I. Cloze Quiz

Chapter 4: Why So Many More Americans Die in Fires

Read the passage on this page. Fill in the blanks below with one word from the list. Use each word once.

attitude	entirely	fighting	neither	successes
country	experts	just	preventing	technology
destroy	fatal	kill	progress	ways
enough	fault	lessons	rates	worst

In some _____ (1), the United States has made spectacular

_____ (2). Fires no longer _____ (3) 18,000 buildings as

they did in the Great Chicago Fire of 1871, or _____ (4) half a town

of 2,400 people, as they did the same night in Peshtigo, Wisconsin.

But even with such _____ (5), the United States still has one of

the _____ (6) fire death _____ (7) in the world. Safety

_____ (8) say the problem is _____ (9) money nor

_____ (10), but the indifference of a _____ (11) that

_____ (12) will not take fires seriously _____ (13).

American fire departments spend far less on _____ (14) fires

than on _____ (15) them. And American fire-safety

_____ (16) are aimed almost _____ (17) at children.

Experts say the _____ (18) error is an _____ (19) that

fires are not really anyone's _____ (20).

Acupuncture: The New Old Medicine
Edited by William G. Flanagan
Forbes

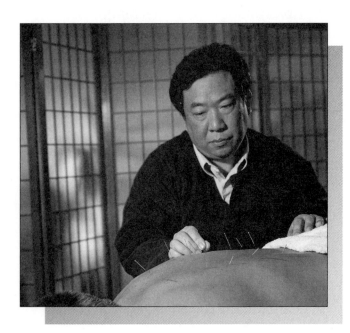

Prereading Preparation

1. What do you know about **acupuncture?** How is it done? Is it a new kind of medicine?

2. Why do people get acupuncture treatments?

3. Have you ever had acupuncture treatments, or do you know someone who has? Describe the experience and the reason for the treatment.

4. Acupuncture is a traditional form of medicine. Do you know of some other traditional kinds of medicine? Are these treatments different from more "modern" medical treatments? How?

5. Read the title of this chapter. Why is acupuncture called the "new old medicine"?

The thin, extremely sharp needles didn't hurt at all going in. Dr. Gong pricked them into my left arm, around the elbow that had been bothering me. Other needles were slipped into my left wrist and, strangely, my *right* arm, and then into both my closed eyelids.

There wasn't any discomfort, just a mild warming sensation, when the electrodes were connected to the needles in my left arm, and my muscles began to twitch involuntarily. However, I did begin to wonder what had driven me here, to the office of Dr. James Gong, a floor up from Mott Street in New York's Chinatown.

Then I remembered—the excruciating pain in that left elbow. Several trips to a Fifth Avenue neurologist and two expensive, uncomfortable medical tests had failed to produce even a diagnosis. "Maybe you lean on your left arm too much," the neurologist concluded, suggesting I see a bone doctor.

During the hours spent waiting in vain to see an orthopedist, I decided to take another track and try acupuncture. A Chinese-American friend recommended Dr. Gong. I took the subway to Canal Street and walked past the open-air fish stalls, the incense shops, the Asia Bank branch, and restaurants with cooked ducks hanging in their windows. Reaching Dr. Gong's second-floor office, marked with a hand painted sign, I felt I could have been in old Hong Kong.

Dr. Gong speaks English, but not often. Most of my questions to him were greeted with a friendly laugh, but I managed to let him know where my arm hurt. He hustled me into a room, had me lie down on a cot, and went to work. In the next room, I learned, a woman dancer was also getting a treatment. As I lay there a while, becoming oblivious to the needles and the muscle spasms and the electric current shooting through my arm, I drifted into a dreamlike state and fantasized about what she looked like.

Not every acupuncturist offers such fantasy trips to China and beyond along with the price of treatment, of course. Acupuncturists today are as likely to be found on Park Avenue as on Mott Street, and they are as likely to be Caucasian as Asian. In all there are an estimated 10,000 acupuncturists in the country, 6,500 of whom are certified one way or another. Nowadays, a lot of M.D.s have learned acupuncture techniques; so have a number of dentists. Reason? Patient demand. Few, though, can adequately explain how acupuncture works.

Acupuncturists may say that the body has more than 800 acupuncture points. A life force called *qi* (pronounced CHEE) circulates through the body. Points on the skin are energetically connected to specific organs, body structures and systems. Acupuncture points are stimulated to balance the circulation of *qi*. It's all very confusing.

The truth is, though acupuncture is at least 2,200 years old, "nobody really knows what's happening," says Paul Zmiewski, a Ph.D. in Chinese studies who practices acupuncture in Philadelphia.

Millions of Americans now seek out the services of acupuncturists, usually because conventional medicine failed to cure their ills. Jack Tymann, 51, president and general manager of Westinghouse Electronic Systems Co., is typical. Tymann was bothered for 15 years with severe lower back pain. His doctor suggested disc surgery, but he decided to try acupuncture instead.

A scientists and an engineer by education, Tymann was highly skeptical at first. "I went in with that symptom, and haven't had any trouble with my back since," he says. He still goes for treatments, four or five times per year—not for back pain, but as a preventive measure. "It's been my primary form of health care for about nine years now," he says.

Harwood Beville, 51, executive vice president of the Rouse Co., started acupuncture nine years ago, for treatment of "what I'll call tennis shoulder." The shoulder had bothered him for two years, and visits to other doctors met with no success. Acupuncture had worked for his wife. After a few treatments, his pain was gone, and there were other noticeable effects. "Immediately, stress didn't seem to be bothering me so much." Like Tymann, he, too, still goes for regular treatments.

Acupuncture is used to treat a variety of ailments—anxiety, depression, back pain, smoking, high blood pressure, stress, arthritis; the list goes on. Acupuncture is even used to help treat drug addiction—with considerable success.

The number of treatments can vary, although one-shot cures are relatively rare. It usually takes four to six sessions to treat a specific ailment. If that doesn't work, you will probably feel at least somewhat better. After five treatments from Dr. Gong, there has been dramatic improvement in my arm, and the pain is a fraction of what it was. I feel less stress, too. I think. The mainly silent Dr. Gong finally even offered a diagnosis for what ailed me. "Pinched nerve," he said.

Fact-Finding Exercise

Read the passage once. Then read the following statements. Scan the article quickly to find out if each statement is true (T) or false (F). If a statement is false, change it so that it is true.

1. ____ T ____ F   Dr. Gong is a neurologist.

   _____

2. ____ T ____ F   The neurologist was not able to stop the author's pain.

   _____

3. ____ T ____ F   Dr. Gong's office is on Fifth Avenue.

   _____

4. ____ T ____ F   Dr. Gong does not know how to speak English.

   _____

5. ____ T ____ F   It is hard to explain how acupuncture works.

   _____

6. ____ T ____ F   Jack Tymann continues to visit an acupuncturist because his back still hurts.

   _____

7. ____ T ____ F   Most acupuncture treatments take more than one session.

   _____

Read each question carefully. Circle the number or letter or the correct answer, or write your answer in the space provided.

1. In the first paragraph, what is a synonym for **pricked into?**

   _____

2. In lines 7–9, the author writes, "However, I did begin to wonder **what had driven me** here, to the office of Dr. Gong." This means that the author was thinking about
   a. how he had gotten there
   b. why he had gone there
   c. what Dr. Gong does

3. Read lines 10–12: "Several trips to a Fifth Avenue neurologist and two expensive, uncomfortable medical tests had **failed to produce a diagnosis.**" **Failed to produce a diagnosis** means that
   a. the author did not pass his medical tests
   b. the tests did not relieve his pain
   c. the tests did not uncover his physical problem

4. In lines 12–13, the neurologist suggested that the author see a bone doctor. In the next paragraph, what is a synonym for **bone doctor?**

   _____

5. Read lines 14–15: "During the hours spent waiting **in vain** to see an orthopedist, I decided to try acupuncture." **In vain** means
   a. uselessly
   b. carefully
   c. quietly

6. In line 23, the author writes, "A woman dancer was also getting a treatment." What does **treatment** mean?

   _____

7. In line 29, what are **Park Avenue** and **Mott Street?**
   a. Similar places
   b. Different places
   c. Medical places

8. Read lines 30–31. "**In all** there are an estimated 10,000 acupuncturists in the country." What does **in all** mean?
   a. In total
   b. In fact
   c. In New York

9. Read lines 31–34: "**Nowadays,** a lot of **M.D.s** have learned acupuncture techniques; so have a number of dentists. Reason? Patient demand. **Few,** though, can adequately explain how acupuncture works."
   a. What does **nowadays** refer to?
      1. Only at the present time
      2. From some time in the past up to the present
      3. During the time that the author's story takes place
   b. What are **M.D.s?**
      1. Doctors
      2. Dentists
      3. Acupuncturists
   c. In line 33, who does **few** refer to?
      1. Only patients
      2. Only M.D.s
      3. Dentists and M.D.s
      4. Only dentists

10. Read line 36: "A life force called **qi** (pronounced CHEE) circulates through the body."
    a. What is **qi?**

    _____

    b. How do you know?

    _____

11. Read lines 44–46: "Jack Tymann, 51, president and general manager of Westinghouse Electronic Systems Co., is typical." This sentence means that Jack Tymann is

   a. a common man
   b. a common example
   c. a common acupuncturist

12. Read lines 46–47: "His doctor suggested disc surgery, but he decided to try acupuncture **instead.**"

   a. Jack Tymann had

      1. surgery, but not acupuncture
      2. surgery and acupuncture
      3. acupuncture, but not surgery

   b. Complete the following sentence correctly.

      Jack and Helen wanted to go to the beach, but it was raining. They decided to

      1. go to the movies instead
      2. go for a walk instead
      3. go for a swim instead

13. Read lines 53–54: "Harwood Beville, 51, executive vice president of the Rouse Co., started acupuncture nine years ago, for treatment of 'what I'll call tennis shoulder.'" How old was Harwood Beville when he started acupuncture?

   a. 51
   b. 42
   c. 60

14. Read lines 60–63: "Acupuncture is used to treat a variety of **ailments**— anxiety, depression, back pain, smoking, high blood pressure, stress, arthritis; the list goes on." What are **ailments?**

   a. Treatments
   b. Problems
   c. Illnesses

C. Word Forms

Part 1

In English, verbs can change to nouns in several ways. Some verbs become nouns by adding the suffix *-ion* or *-tion,* for example, *prevent (v.), prevention (n.).* Complete each sentence with the correct form of the words on the left. **Use the correct tense of the verbs, in either the affirmative or the negative form. Use the singular or plural form of the nouns.**

explain *(v.)*
explanation *(n.)*

1. a. Yesterday, the teacher _____ how electricity is produced because she didn't have time.
    b. Tomorrow, when she gives her scientific _____, I will take notes.

recommend *(v.)*
recommendation *(n.)*

2. a. John _____ that I take advanced calculus this semester, but I didn't listen to him.
    b. I should have taken his advice because his _____ have always been sensible.

stimulate *(v.)*
stimulation *(n.)*

3. a. Babies need constant _____ in order to help their development.
    b. If adults _____ babies' interest in the world around them, they will become more alert.

conclude *(v.)*
conclusion *(n.)*

4. a. Copernicus, a well-known Polish astronomer, _____ that the Earth was round.
    b. He reached his revolutionary _____ in the sixteenth century.

decide *(v.)*
decision *(n.)*

5. a. I _____ yet where to apply to graduate school.
    b. I need to make some other important _____ first, such as whether to stay in this country or go back home.

In English, adjectives usually become adverbs by adding the suffix -ly, for example, *immediate (adj.), immediately (adv.).*

Complete each sentence with the correct form of the words on the left.

extreme *(adj.)*
extremely *(adv.)*

1. a. Some people believe that the death penalty is an _____ form of punishment.
    b. Others believe that murder is an _____ serious crime, and that murderers deserve capital punishment.

strange *(adj.)*
strangely *(adv.)*

2. a. Barbara has been acting very _____ lately. I wonder if anything is wrong.
    b. Perhaps I should ask her about her _____ behavior.

involuntary *(adj.)*
involuntarily *(adv.)*

3. a. Sometimes people jump when they hear thunder. This is called an _____ reaction.
    b. Other people react _____ when they see something unexpectedly.

adequate *(adj.)*
adequately *(adv.)*

4. a. This essay is clearly not _____. It should be at least 300 words.
    b. You cannot express your point of view _____ in only 100 words.

usual *(adj.)*
usually *(adv.)*

5. a. Eve _____, but not always, takes her vacation in August.
    b. This is because her _____ vacation consists of relaxing on the beach and swimming in the ocean.

D. DICTIONARY SKILLS

Choose the appropriate definition for each word. Then write the number and the synonym or meaning in the space provided. **Be sure to use the correct form of the verbs and nouns.**

1.

> **conclude** *v* **1** come or bring to an end: *He ~d by saying that . . .* **2** arrange; bring about: *to ~ a treaty with . . .* **3** arrive at a belief or opinion: *The jury ~d from the evidence, that the accused man was not guilty.*

The neurologist (___)_____ that perhaps I leaned on my left arm too much and suggested that I see a bone doctor.

2.

> **hustle** *v* **1** push or shove roughly: *The police ~d the thief into their van.* **2** hurry; rush: *I don't want to ~ you into a decision.* **3** (*informal*) sell or obtain something by energetic (and sometimes illegal) activity.

Dr. Gong (___)_____ me into a room, had me lie down on a cot, and went to work.

3.

> **fail** *v* **1** be unsuccessful: *All our plans ~ed.* **2** grade (a student) as failing in a course, an examination, etc: *Students not taking the final exam will be ~ed.* **3** be not enough; come to an end while still needed or expected: *The crops ~ed because of drought.* **4** omit; neglect: *He never ~s to write (= always writes) to his mother every week.*

Millions of Americans go to acupuncturists, usually because conventional medicine (___)_____. It does not cure their ills.

4.

> **dramatic** *adj* **1** of drama: *~ performance.* **2** sudden or exciting: *~ changes in the international situation.* **3** (of a person, his speech, behavior) showing feelings or character in a lively way.

After five treatments from Dr. Gong, there has been (___)_____ improvement in my arm.

Information Organization

Read the article a second time. Underline what you think are the main ideas. Then scan the article and complete the following outline, using the sentences that you have underlined to help you. You will use this outline later to answer specific questions about the article.

I.   The Author's Thoughts About His First Acupuncture Experience
   A. How the treatment felt
      1.
      2.
   B. Why he had come to Dr. Gong's office
      1.
      2.

II. A Description of Today's Acupuncturists
   A.
   B.
   C.

III. A Description of Acupuncture
   A.
   B. A life force called *qi* (pronounced CHEE) circulates through the body
   C.
   D.
   E. Acupuncture is at least 2,200 years old, but nobody really knows how it works

IV. Who Gets Acupuncture Treatments
   A. number of people:
     usual reason:
   B. examples of people who have acupuncture treatments:
      1.
      2.

V. Uses of Acupuncture
    A.
    B.

VI. Effectiveness of Acupuncture
    A.

Read each question carefully. Use your notes to answer the questions. Do not refer back to the text. Write your answers in the space provided under each question. When you are finished, write a brief summary of the article.

1. Why did the author decide to go to an acupuncturist?

   _____

   _____

   _____

2. What is acupuncture? How does it work?

   _____

   _____

   _____

3. a. Why did Jack Tymann go to an acupuncturist? What was the result of his treatments?

   _____

   _____

   _____

   b. Why did Harwood Beville go to an acupuncturist? What was the result of his treatments?

   _____

   _____

   _____

4. What can acupuncturists treat?

   _____

   _____

   _____

5. How long do acupuncture treatments usually take?

_____

_____

_____

Summary

_____

_____

_____

_____

_____

G. *Critical Thinking Strategies*

Reach each question carefully. Write your response in the space provided. Remember that there is no one correct answer. Your response depends on what **you** think.

1. In the first paragraph of this passage, the author describes his acupuncture treatment. He writes, "Other needles were slipped into my left wrist and, strangely, my right arm, and then into both my closed eyelids." Why did he think this was strange?

   _____

   _____

   _____

   _____

2. In lines 10–12, the author talks about his experiences with a "Fifth Avenue neurologist." What do you think the author believed about Fifth Avenue doctors before he had acupuncture treatments?

   _____

   _____

   _____

   _____

3. In the third paragraph, the author describes his experience with the Fifth Avenue neurologist. In the fourth paragraph, he recounts his trip to Dr. Gong's office. The author gives different impressions about the two doctors and their environments. What are they?

   _____

   _____

   _____

   _____

4. According to this article, Harwood Beville went to an acupuncturist because other doctors could not help him and because "acupuncture had worked for his wife." How do you think Mrs. Beville's experience affected Mr. Beville?

_____

_____

_____

_____

5. Read the last two sentences of this article. What is the tone of these statements? In other words, what is the author's opinion about Dr. Gong?

_____

_____

_____

_____

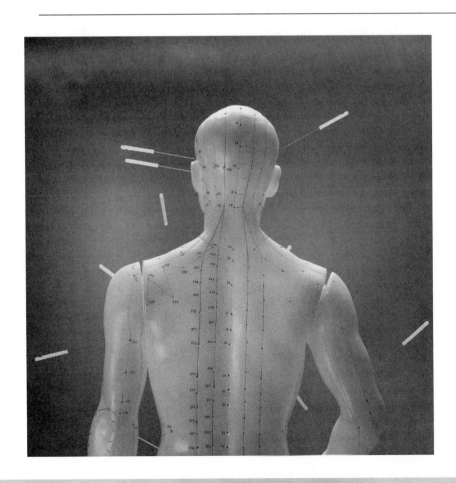

H. *Follow-up Discussion* AND *Writing Activities*

1. **Jigsaw Reading:** You are going to read more information about acupuncture: what it is, how it works, and what it treats.

   a. First, all students read the paragraph titled *Acupuncture*. Discuss it in class to make sure everyone understands it.

   b. Second, work in a group of three or four students. Each group will read different information about acupuncture on the following pages. Group A will read about what acupuncture is; Group B will read about how acupuncture works; Group C will read about what acupuncture treats. If your class is large, then you may have more than one Group A, B, or C; just make sure that at least one group reads about each segment on acupuncture. After reading the paragraph, discuss it to make sure everyone in the group understands about their particular segment.

   c. Third, set up different groups so that each group has a student or students who have read each paragraph. In these new groups, tell each other what you have read about acupuncture. In the spaces under your paragraph, take notes about the information the other students give you. Do not look back at your readings. Ask each other questions to make sure that all the students in your group understand all the information about acupuncture.

   d. Finally, work together to answer the questions on pages 100–101. When your group is finished, compare your answers with the other groups' answers.

All Students Read: *Acupuncture*

Acupuncture is a scientific and complete system based on exact laws and principles. It has been used in China for centuries. In fact, classical Chinese acupuncture is one of the oldest forms of medicine known to humankind.

Group A Only: *What Is Acupuncture?*

Acupuncture is a system of medicine used to restore and maintain health, as well as prevent illness. It originated in China over 5,000 years ago and is based on the belief that any illness or symptom is associated with an imbalance in the body's vital life energy. Traditional acupuncture works to restore the natural flow of this energy throughout the body, relieving the underlying cause of the illness and the accompanying symptoms.

Group B's Information:

_____

_____

_____

_____

_____

_____

_____

Group C's Information:

_____

_____

_____

_____

_____

_____

_____

_____

_____

The vital energy, known as "qi" energy, travels in twelve pathways called "meridians." Each meridian corresponds to a vital organ, such as kidneys, liver, heart, stomach, lungs, etc. Each has a pulse that informs the acupuncturist of the condition of the energy within that meridian. When the acupuncturist inserts very fine needles into points that lie along these meridians, energy is summoned to the places that need it and dispersed from the areas where it is congested. In this way the natural flow of energy along the pathways is restored and healthy patterns reestablished over time.

Group A's Information:

_____

_____

_____

_____

_____

_____

_____

Group C's Information:

_____

_____

_____

_____

_____

_____

_____

Group C Only: *What Does Acupuncture Treat?*

Acupuncture treats the whole person—the body, the mind, and the spirit—therefore, it can be helpful in the treatment of all conditions. In addition to its widespread use in the relief of pain, acupuncture has been used to treat a wide variety of illnesses both as a primary modality and as an adjunct to traditional western medicine. Acupuncture is useful in treating chronic conditions, e.g., headaches, chronic fatigue, anxiety, and insomnia. It increases energy levels, assists the immune system, and contributes to a person's general well-being.

Group A's Information:

_____

_____

_____

_____

_____

_____

_____

Group B's Information:

_____

_____

_____

_____

_____

_____

_____

1. What is acupuncture?

    _____

    _____

2. When did it originate?

    _____

    _____

3. What belief is acupuncture based on?

    _____

    _____

4. What is "Ch'i" *(qi)* energy?

    _____

    _____

5. What is a meridian?

    _____

    _____

6. How is acupuncture done?

    _____

    _____

7. How does acupuncture help the patient?

    _____

    _____

8. How does acupuncture treat the whole person?

_____

_____

9. What illnesses does acupuncture help?

_____

_____

10. What other problems does acupuncture treat?

_____

_____

H. *Follow-up Discussion* AND *Writing Activities* (continued)

2. Many people today are using traditional forms of medicine in place of modern treatments. What do you think are some reasons for this change? Write a composition to explain your answer.

3. a. In a group, make a list of common illnesses. Next to each illness, write the traditional forms of medicine that you know are used to treat these illnesses, both in your country and in other countries. Then write the modern treatments for these illnesses. Compare the two types of treatments for each illness you have chosen. For instance, which treatment is usually less expensive? Which usually takes less time to see positive results? Which seems to be more effective? Which is less extreme, i.e., involves taking medicine or getting therapy, as opposed to having surgery?

   b. For each illness, discuss which type of treatment you would prefer if you had that illness. Explain your reasons to your classmates.

   c. As a class, list on the blackboard all the illnesses that you discussed and the traditional and modern treatments for each. Then take a poll to see how many students prefer the traditional treatments and how many students prefer the modern treatments for these ailments.

4. **Write in your journal.** Select a traditional form of medicine that has been used in your country for a long time. Describe its uses and its effectiveness. Discuss your personal experience with this traditional form or the experience of someone you know. Tell whether you would recommend this form of medicine to others, and why.

Cloze Quiz

Chapter 5: Acupuncture: The New Old Medicine

Read the passage on this page. Fill in the blanks below with one word from the list. Use each word once.

acupuncture	doctors	president	since	symptom
bothered	education	preventive	skeptical	treatments
conventional	instead	primary	success	typical
cure	pain	services	suggested	visits

Millions of Americans now seek out the ＿＿＿＿＿＿＿＿ of
(1)

acupuncturists, usually because ＿＿＿＿＿＿＿＿ medicine failed to
(2)

＿＿＿＿＿＿＿＿ their ills. Jack Tymann, 51, is ＿＿＿＿＿＿＿＿. Tymann
(3)   (4)

was ＿＿＿＿＿＿＿＿ for 15 years with severe lower back pain. His doctor
(5)

＿＿＿＿＿＿＿＿ disc surgery, but he decided to try acupuncture
(6)

＿＿＿＿＿＿＿＿. A scientist and an engineer by ＿＿＿＿＿＿＿＿,
(7)   (8)

Tymann was highly ＿＿＿＿＿＿＿＿ at first. "I went in with that
(9)

＿＿＿＿＿＿＿＿ and haven't had any trouble with my back
(10)

＿＿＿＿＿＿＿＿," he says. He still goes for ＿＿＿＿＿＿＿＿ four or five
(11)   (12)

times per year—not for back pain, but as a ＿＿＿＿＿＿＿＿ measure. "It's
(13)

been my ＿＿＿＿＿＿＿＿ form of health care for about nine years now,"
(14)

he says.

Harwood Beville, 51, executive vice ＿＿＿＿＿＿＿＿ of the Rouse Co.,
(15)

started ＿＿＿＿＿＿＿＿ nine years ago. His shoulder had bothered him for
(16)

two years, and ＿＿＿＿＿＿＿＿ to other ＿＿＿＿＿＿＿＿ met with no
(17)   (18)

＿＿＿＿＿＿＿＿. After a few treatments, his ＿＿＿＿＿＿＿＿ was gone.
(19)   (20)

Highs and Lows in Self-Esteem
by Kim Lamb Gregory
Scripps Howard News Service

Prereading Preparation

1. Look at the photograph. How do the people in the photo feel about themselves?

2. Work alone. Complete the following chart. How did you feel about yourself at each stage of your life? Was your self-esteem high or low?

Childhood	Adolescence	Young Adulthood	Adult

3. Work in a small group. Compare your answers in the chart. Did you all have the same level of self-esteem at the same stages of your life?

Highs and Lows in Self-Esteem

1   No one in the Gould family of Westlake Village, California, was surprised
2 by a study suggesting a person's age and stage of life may have a bigger impact on
3 self-esteem than we ever realized. A study of about 350,000 people likens a
4 person's self-esteem across the human lifespan to a roller coaster ride, starting
5 with an inflated sense of self-approval in late childhood that plunges in
6 adolescence. Self-esteem rises steadily though adulthood, only to drop to its
7 lowest point ever in old age. "I've gone through pretty much all of those cycles,"
8 Fred Gould said. At 60, he's edging toward retirement. Fred's wife, Eileen, 46,
9 is a businesswoman in the throes of mid-adulthood and, according to the study,
10 predisposed to a healthy self-regard. At 21, the Goulds' son, Jeff, has just
11 launched that heady climb into adulthood and a buoyant self-regard after an
12 adolescence fraught with the usual perils of self-doubt and hormonal warfare.
13 His sister, Aly, 17, disagrees with a lot of the study, believing instead that each
14 individual has an intrinsic sense of self-esteem that remains relatively constant.
15 But she does agree that adolescence can give even the most solid sense of self-
16 esteem a sound battering. "As a teenager, I can definitely speak for all of us
17 when I say we bag on ourselves." Aly said.

The Study

18   The drop in self-esteem in adolescence was no surprise to Richard Robins,
19 a psychology professor at the University of California at Davis, who spearheaded
20 the study, but "the drop in old age is a little bit more novel," he said.
21 Specifically, Robins was intrigued by the similarities in self-esteem levels
22 between those entering adolescence and old age. "There is an accumulation of
23 losses occurring all at once both in old age and adolescence," he suggested.
24 "There is a critical mass of transition going on."
25   Those answering the survey ranged in age from 9 to 90. They participated
26 in the survey by logging onto a Web site during a period between 1999 and
27 2000. About three-quarters were Caucasian, the rest a mixture of people of
28 Asian, black, Latino and Middle-Eastern descent. Most were from the United
29 States. The survey simply asked people to agree or strongly disagree—on a five-
30 point scale—with the statement: "I see myself as someone who has high self-
31 esteem."
32   Everybody is an individual, Robins stressed, so self-esteem can be affected
33 by a number of things that are biological, social, and situational, but there are
35 certain passages that all of us face—and each passage can have a powerful effect

on our sense of self. "With kids, their feelings about themselves are often based on relatively superficial information," Robins explained. "As we get older, we base our self-esteem on actual achievements and feedback from other people."

Overall, the study indicated that women do not fare as well as men in self-esteem—a difference particularly marked in adolescence. "During adolescence, girls' self-esteem dropped about twice as much as boys'," Robins said, perhaps at least partially because of society's heavy emphasis on body image for girls. Add one negative life event to all of this turmoil, and a teenager's delicate self-esteem can crumble.

Emerging into Adulthood

Eileen remembered having fairly high self-esteem from ages 12 to 16. She had been very ill as a child, so the teen years were a time for her to blossom. Then, her mother died when she was 17, and her self-esteem bottomed out. "I was like, 'What do I do? How do I handle this?'" Eileen remembered. Eileen was 22 when she married Fred, an event that coincided with the beginning of her adult years—and an upswing in her self-esteem. Like many adults, Eileen gained her senses of competence and continuity, both of which can contribute to the rise in self-esteem during the adult years, Robins said.

Even if there is divorce or some other form of chaos, there has been a change in our ability to cope, he said. We learn with experience. Fred is aware that his sense of self-esteem may be vulnerable when he retires. "I'm concerned about keeping my awareness level," he said. "Am I going to be aware of the social scene? Of things more global? Am I going to be able to read and keep up with everything?"

Seniors do tend to experience a drop in self-esteem when they get into their 70s, the study says—but not always. This is enigmatic to Robins. "When we look at things like general well-being, the evidence is mixed about what happens in old age," he said.

Some people experience a tremendous loss of self-esteem, whereas others maintain their sense of well-being right through old age. Others are not as lucky. Whereas adolescents lose their sense of childhood omnipotence, seniors experience another kind of loss. Retirement comes at about the same time seniors may begin to lose loved ones, their health, their financial status, or their sense of competence. Suddenly, someone who was so in charge may become withdrawn, sullen, and depressed. Their self-esteem may plummet. Robins hopes the study will makes us more aware of the times when our self-esteem can be in jeopardy.

Fact-Finding Exercise

Read the passage again. Read the following statements. Check whether they are true (T) or false (F). If a statement is false, rewrite the statement so that it is true.

1. ____ T ____ F   A person's self-esteem is high during childhood.

   _____

2. ____ T ____ F   A person's self-esteem does not change during adolescence.

   _____

3. ____ T ____ F   A person experiences the lowest self-esteem during old age.

   _____

4. ____ T ____ F   The people in the study were mostly Asian.

   _____

5. ____ T ____ F   Our self-esteem is affected by several factors.

   _____

6. ____ T ____ F   Our self-esteem is most delicate when we are adults.

   _____

7. ____ T ____ F   Older people's self-esteem always drops when they get into their 70s.

   _____

Read each question carefully. Circle the number or letter of the correct answer, or write your answer in the space provided.

1. Read the first paragraph. The author compares the changes in a person's self-esteem over a lifetime to a roller coaster ride. How does the author think a person's self-esteem changes during a lifetime?

    a. It continues to rise throughout the person's life.
    b. It begins high, but decreases throughout a person's life.
    c. It begins high, then gets lower and higher throughout a person's life.

2. Read lines 3–6. **Likens** means

    a. enjoys
    b. compares
    c. excites

3. In the first paragraph, which word is a synonym for **plunge?**

    _____

4. Read line 8. **Edging toward** means

    a. becoming sharper
    b. moving close to
    c. getting older

5. Read lines 10–12. **Launched** means

    a. begun
    b. finished
    c. dropped

6. Read lines 13–14. Aly believes that teenagers

    a. feel good about themselves
    b. have negative feelings about themselves
    c. have high self-esteem

7. Read lines 18–20.

   a. **Spearheaded** means
      1. led
      2. attacked
      3. joined

   b. Robins said that "the drop in old age is a little bit more **novel.**" He means that the drop in self-esteem in old age is more
      1. like a book
      2. unusual
      3. expected

8. Read lines 22–24.

   a. **Accumulation** means
      1. building up
      2. series of
      3. number of

   b. **Transition** means
      1. unhappiness
      2. change
      3. aging

9. Read line 25. **Those** refers to

   a. the people who responded to the survey
   b. the people who wrote the survey
   c. the people who mailed out the survey

10. In lines 35–37, **superficial information** and **actual achievements** are

   a. opposite ideas
   b. similar ideas

11. Read lines 38–41. **Fare** means

   a. work
   b. manage
   c. grow

12. Read lines 44–46.

    a. **Blossom** means

        1. develop well
        2. grow flowers
        3. get taller

    b. **Bottom out** means

        1. disappear completely
        2. reach a very low point
        3. change greatly

13. Read lines 48–51. Which word in these sentences is a synonym of **upswing?**

    _____

14. Read lines 64–67. Which one of the following statements is true?

    a. Both adolescents and seniors experience the same sense of loss.
    b. Adolescents experience a sense of loss, but seniors do not.
    c. Adolescents and seniors experience a different sense of loss.

15. In line 70, **in jeopardy** means

    a. in danger
    b. about to change
    c. in question

Part 1

In English, some verbs change to nouns by adding *-tion* or *-ion,* for example, *collect (v.), collection (n.).*

Complete each sentence with a correct form of the words on the left. Be careful of spelling changes. **Use the correct tense of the verb in either the affirmative or the negative form. Use the singular or plural form of the nouns.**

contribute *(v.)*   1.   a.   John always _____ to class discussions.
contribution *(n.)*   b.   His thoughtful _____ are always interesting.

participate *(v.)*   2.   a.   Janet _____ in the school play next week.
participation *(n.)*   b.   She is sorry about her lack of _____, but she has to go out of town for an interview.

accumulate *(v.)*   3.   a.   Susan has a surprising _____ of newspapers in her basement.
accumulation *(n.)*   b.   She _____ so many newspapers because she never throws them out. It's a real fire hazard!

realize *(v.)*   4.   a.   I _____ how hard Maria works until last week.
realization *(n.)*   b.   I came to this _____ when I spent the day with her in her office.

suggest *(v.)*   5.   a.   Michelle wanted to get a full-time job, but her friend _____ that she wait until she finishes school.
suggestion *(n.)*   b.   Michelle listened to her friend's _____. She finished school, and then went to work full time.

In English, the verb and noun forms of some words are the same, for example, *experience (n.)* and *experience (v.)*.

Complete each sentence with the correct form of the word on the left. **Use the correct tense of the verb in either the affirmative or the negative form. Use the singular or plural form of the noun. In addition, indicate whether you are using the noun *(n.)* or verb *(v.)* form.**

drop

1. a. During the night, the temperature _____ by 30
       (n., v.)
       degrees. It was only 26 degrees outside when we woke up!

   b. The sudden _____ in temperature had not been
       (n., v.)
       predicted, so we were all very surprised.

gain

2. a. Harry practiced the piano every day. Over several
       months, he _____ considerable skill and confidence.
                    (n., v.)

   b. Because of Harry's _____ in both skill and
                          (n., v.)
       confidence, he was able to play in public.

plunge

3. a. The newspaper predicted a tremendous _____ in
                                              (n., v.)
       oil prices over the next several months.

   b. Because oil prices _____ recently, the price of
                          (n., v.)
       gasoline dropped, too.

survey

4. a. When Anna planned her detailed _____ on self-
                                       (n., v.)
       esteem, she did not include children under the age of 12.

   b. She _____ younger children because she was
          (n., v.)
       uncomfortable asking them such personal questions.

range

5. a. The students in my school come from a wide _____
                                                   (n., v.)
       of countries and speak numerous languages.

   b. The languages they speak _____ from Korean,
                                (n., v.)
       Japanese, Mandarin, Cantonese, Tagalog, and Vietnamese
       to Hindi, Farsi, German, French, and Spanish.

D. DICTIONARY SKILLS

Read the dictionary entry for each word. Indicate the number of the definition and write the synonym or meaning in the space provided. Remember that you may need to change the wording of the definition in order to have a grammatically correct sentence.

1.
> **impact** *n* **1** a forceful contact, blow: *The meteor made a large impact when it crashed to earth.* **2** effect, impression: *Poverty has a bad impact on people's health.*

A study suggested that a person's age and stage of life may have a bigger (___)_____on self-esteem than we ever realized.

2.
> **inflate** *v* **1** to fill with air: *A mechanic inflated the car's tires.* **2** to raise above the normal or proper level: *During shortages, some merchants inflate prices.* **3** *fig.* to pump up, swell: *Praise inflates his ego.*

A study of about 350,000 people likens a person's self-esteem across the human lifespan to a roller coaster ride, starting with an (___)_____ sense of self-approval in late childhood that plunges in adolescence.

3.
> **scale** *n* **1** an instrument for weighing things: *I weighed six apples on the scale.*‖*According to the scale, I've lost four pounds.* **2** a system of measurement or comparison: *On a scale of 1 to 10, I rate this film a 7, quite good.* **3** on a map, a small chart that shows the actual distance: *The scale for this map is 1 inch equals 100 miles.* **4** (in music) a set of notes with the same interval between each one: *She played a C-major scale on the piano.* **5** a section of the skin on a fish or a reptile: *a fish scale* **6 on a large** or **small scale:** in a big or small way: *In a big city like New York, people think of life on a large scale.*‖*The jeweler works on a small scale, with tiny tools.*

The survey asked people to agree or strongly disagree—on a 5-point (___)_____ with the statement "I see myself as someone who has high self-esteem."

4.
> **vulnerable** *adj* **1** exposed, unprotected:
> *The soldiers were in a position vulnerable to*
> *attack by the enemy.* **2** likely to be hurt or
> made to feel bad: *She has been feeling very*
> *vulnerable since her husband died.*

Fred is aware that his sense of self-esteem may be
(   )_____ when he retires.

The author compares the stages of self-esteem to a roller-coaster ride. Turn your book and write the different stages of a person's self-esteem in the arrows on the chart below. Then write some reasons for each stage.

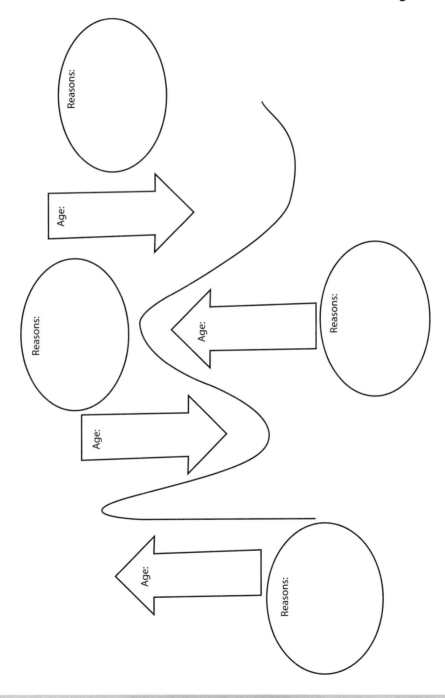

Read each question carefully. Use your chart to answer the questions. Do not refer back to the text. Write your answers in the space provided under each question. When you are finished, write a brief summary of the article.

1. What are the different stages of self-esteem that most people go through?

   a. _____

   b. _____

   c. _____

   d. _____

2. For each stage, what happens in people's lives to cause these changes in self-esteem?

   a. _____

   _____

   b. _____

   _____

   c. _____

   _____

   d. _____

   _____

Summary

_____

_____

_____

_____

_____

G. Critical Thinking Strategies

Read each question carefully. Write your response in the space provided. Remember that there is no one correct answer. Your response depends on what **you** think.

1. The author states that "There is an accumulation of losses occurring all at once both in old age and adolescence." What losses do you think occur at these two stages of our lives? Why do you think so?

   _____

   _____

   _____

2. According to Richard Robins, we all face certain passages at different times in our lives. What might some of these passages be for adolescents? For adults? Why do these passages occur at these particular points in our lives?

   _____

   _____

   _____

3. In terms of self-esteem, adolescent girls do not manage as well as adolescent boys. Why is body image such a focus for girls, as opposed to boys? Is this focus beginning to change for boys? Why or why not?

   _____

   _____

   _____

4. Richard Robins describes Eileen's experiences (lines 44–51) as a young girl emerging into adulthood. Are her experiences a good example of the kinds of changes that most adolescents go through? Why or why not?

   _____

   _____

   _____

5. At the end of the article, Robins hopes that this study will make us more aware of times when our self-esteem may be in danger. Why might this be important for us to know?

_____

_____

_____

H. *Follow-up Discussion* AND *Writing Activities*

1. According to Richard Robins, self-esteem is affected by biological, social, and situational factors. Work with a partner or in a small group. Discuss which biological, social, and situational factors might affect people at each stage of life. Use the chart below to organize your ideas.

	Childhood	Adolescence	Young Adult	Adult
biological factors				
social factors				
situational factors				

2. What are some ways that adolescents can maintain their sense of self-esteem in spite of the losses they experience? What advice would you give an adolescent who is suffering a drop in self-esteem?

3. Seniors experience many losses: they retire, and so lose their jobs; loved ones die; their health may deteriorate. What are some ways that seniors can cope with some of these losses?

4. **Write in your journal.** The author compares the stages of self-esteem in our lives to a roller coaster. Do you think this is an accurate comparison? Why or why not? What analogy would you use to describe your own stages of self-esteem?

Cloze Quiz

Chapter 6: Highs and Lows in Self-Esteem

Read the passage on this page. Fill in the blanks below with one word from the list. Use each word once.

accumulation	bottomed out	fare	passage	spearheaded
adolescence	disagrees	inflated	plunges	survey
adulthood	dropped	launched	self-esteem	transition
blossom	edging	likens	social	upswing

No one in the Gould family of Westlake Village, Calif., was surprised by a study suggesting a person's age and stage of life may have a bigger impact on self-esteem than we ever realized. A study of about 350,000 people

_____ a person's self-esteem across the human lifespan to a
(1)

roller coaster ride, starting with an _____ sense of self-approval
(2)

in late childhood that _____ in adolescence. Self-esteem rises
(3)

steadily through adulthood, only to drop to its lowest point ever in old age.

"I've gone through pretty much all of those cycles," Fred Gould said. At 60,

he's _____ toward retirement. Fred's wife, Eileen, 46, is a
(4)

businesswoman in the throes of mid-adulthood and, according to the study,

predisposed to a healthy self-regard. At 21, the Goulds' son, Jeff, has just

_____ that heady climb into _____ and a buoyant
(5)   (6)

self-regard after an _____ fraught with the usual perils of self-
(7)

doubt and hormonal warfare. His sister, Aly, 17, _____ with a lot
(8)

of the study, believing instead that each individual has an intrinsic sense of

_____ that remains relatively constant. But she does agree that
(9)

adolescence can give even the most solid sense of self-esteem a sound battering.

The Study

The drop in self-esteem in adolescence was no surprise to Richard Robins, a psychology professor at the University of California at Davis who _____ the study, but "the drop in old age is a little bit more
(10)
novel," he said. Specifically, Robins was intrigued by the similarities in self-esteem levels between those entering adolescence and old age. "There is an _____ of losses occurring all at once both in old age and
(11)
adolescence," he suggested. "There is a critical mass of _____
(12)
going on."

Those answering the survey ranged in age from 9 to 90. They participated in the _____ by logging onto a Web site during a
(13)
period between 1999 and 2000. The survey simply asked people to agree or strongly disagree—on a five-point scale—with the statement:"I see myself as someone who has high self-esteem."

Everybody is an individual, Robins stressed, so self-esteem can be affected by a number of things that are biological, _____ and
(14)
situational, but there are certain passages that all of us face—and each _____ can have a powerful effect on our sense of self.
(15)
Overall, the study indicated that women do not _____ as
(16)
well as men in self-esteem—a difference particularly marked in adolescence. "During adolescence, girls' self-esteem _____ about twice as
(17)
much as boys'," Robins said, perhaps at least partially because of society's heavy emphasis on body image for girls. Add one negative life event to all of this turmoil and a teenager's delicate self-esteem can crumble.

Eileen remembered having fairly high self-esteem from ages 12 to 16. She had been very ill as a child, so the teen years were a time for her to

_____. Then, her mother died when she was 17, and her self-
       (18)

esteem _____. "I was like, 'What do I do? How do I handle this?'"
          (19)

Eileen remembered. Eileen was 22 when she married Fred, an event that coincided with the beginning of her adult years—and an _____
                                          (20)

in her self-esteem. Like many adults, Eileen gained her senses of competence and continuity, both of which can contribute to the rise in self-esteem during the adult years, Robins said.

Unit 2 Review

Read the clues on the next page. Write the answers in the correct spaces in the puzzle.

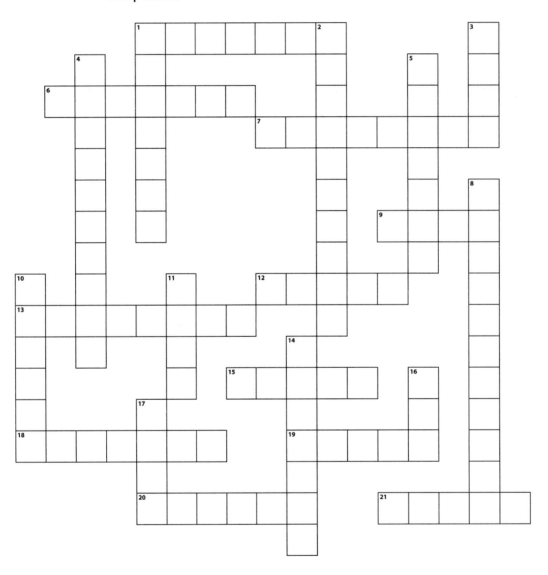

Crossword Clues

Across

1. An _____ is an illness.
6. A small number
7. To arrive at a belief or opinion
9. The past tense of **read**
12. The opposite of **right**
13. Enough; sufficient
15. The crime of deliberately starting a fire
18. Myself, yourself, _____, herself
19. Compare to
20. Ours, yours, _____
21. Unusual

Down

1. When you make a speech, you _____ a group of people.
2. A change
3. The past tense of **ride**
4. Deaths
5. To suddenly drop or plunge
8. The age between 13 and 19 years old
10. To start up
11. To be unsuccessful
14. In vain
16. Ann has one _____ and two daughters.
17. The past tense of **go**

1. Even though we live in a modern world, we are still faced with basic dangers and threats to our physical and mental health, for example, fire, illness, pain, and loss of self-esteem. Discuss what you think is the biggest threat to you. What is the biggest threat to your family? What can you and your family do about these threats?

2. In Chapter 4, people use laws and prevention in order to protect themselves against fire. In Chapter 5, the author turned to acupuncture, a traditional treatment for pain, after modern medical treatments did not work. In Chapter 6, the author discusses many factors involved in loss of self-esteem at different points in our lives, but he does not offer any solutions. What solutions might there be to help prevent loss of self-esteem?

1   The number of house fires in the United States doubles during the month of December. Why do you think this is true? Are these fires caused by arson or by negligence?

2. Match the descriptions about fire safety on the left with the answers on the right. Write the correct letter on the line after the descriptions.

    1. A potentially fatal combination _____   a.   400
    2. Lights that can be used inside or outside _____   b.   Candles
    3. Fires involving Christmas trees _____   c.   Christmas trees
                                                              & holiday lights
    4. About 1/3 purchased at Christmas _____   d.   Wicks of candles
    5. Trim to 1/4 inch _____   e.   Red UL rating

3. What are some steps people in the United States can take to deter fires? What can they learn from other countries about fire prevention?

INFOTRAC® Research Activity
COLLEGE EDITION
The Online Library

Acupuncture is one of several types of alternative medicine that Americans are experimenting with nowadays. Using InfoTrac, type in "acupuncture and medicine" and "acupuncture; newspapers," and read the titles of 20 or 30 articles until you can list at least 10 ailments or problems that acupuncture claims to help. Share your list with a small group of students. Each group member should choose an article on a different ailment or problem to read about in depth and summarize. Pick an article that is at least 300 words long, and write a one-paragraph summary. Read and discuss your summaries with your group and present what you found out about acupuncture to the whole class.

GOVERNMENT AND EDUCATION

The Federal System of Government
by Patricia C. Acheson
from *Our Federal Government: How It Works*

Prereading Preparation

1. How did the United States become an independent country?

2. a. Who were the first Europeans in the United States?

   b. Why did they come to the United States?

3. a. What kind of government does the United States have?

   b. What do you know about this type of government?

4. What is a **constitution?** Why do governments have constitutions? What is their usual purpose?

5. Take a survey in your class. On the blackboard, write the name of the country each student is from. Then, write the type of government each country has. Which countries have the same type of government? Which countries have the same type of government as the United States?

What is the government of the United States exactly? How and when did it come to be? Who were the people who agreed to accept our government and why did they want to accept it?

The answers to these questions lie in the events that took place between 1775 and 1787. In 1775 the war against British domination began. At that point there was no central American government established by law. There was only the Continental Congress made up of men who believed in independence and who were willing to fight for their cause. It was that Congress that declared the colonies independent of Great Britain in July, 1776, and it was only after that decision that the evolution of our present form of government began. The initial step was to establish legal governments in the states to replace colonial rule. The states established republics; each of the thirteen new states had elected governors and representative assemblies.

The Continental Congress was without legal foundation, and it was necessary to establish some form of overall government agreed to by the people and speaking for all the states. However, the Americans of this period reluctantly accepted this necessity, as the majority believed that they could guarantee their freedom only if each state remained almost entirely independent of the others.

Therefore, the first government of the United States under the Articles of Confederation adopted in 1781 was very restricted in its authority. It consisted of a Congress made up of representatives from the states. There was no president with certain specific powers, only a chairman whose job it was to preside and to keep order. The Congress had very little power to do anything. Congress could not pass tax laws; it did not have the sole authority to coin money for use by the states, nor could it regulate trade between the states. Because it had no money of its own, the Congress could not pay any of its debts, it could not borrow money, and it could not pay an army or a navy.

Within four years after the end of the war in 1783, it became obvious that the system of government under the Articles of Confederation was not working out. The discontent and the fact that the new nation was extraordinarily weak without an adequate army or navy made thoughtful people realize that a better government must be worked out if the United States of America was to be a strong and rich nation. In Philadelphia in 1787 a convention, or meeting, was held in order to reshape the government. It was there that our present system of government was born, and the Constitution of the United States was written. The people of the United States are still governed today by the framework drawn up in that document over two hundred years ago.

The Constitution

The foreword to the Constitution stated the democratic principles to be followed by the United States government. The government must insure freedom for the citizens of the United States for all time.

To create such a government was not an easy thing to do. Remember that in 1787 the men at the convention in Philadelphia were pioneers in the setting up of a democratic republican government. They really only knew what they did not want. They did not want a king, and they did not want too strong a central government because they were afraid of losing their own freedoms. They certainly wanted to keep the states as they were. To erase them would have been impossible. Each colony had its own individuality and pride. There could be no question of making just one government and forgetting the individual states. On the other hand, the men in Philadelphia knew that the first government set up under the Articles of Confederation had had too little power to carry out its business, and no one had been satisfied.

Here was a dilemma. On the one hand, it seemed that a strong central government was very undesirable because it might endanger the people's liberties. On the other hand, a weak central government had proven inadequate. The solution these men found is called the "system of checks and balances," and it is the heart and soul of the Constitution.

The System of Checks and Balances

The writers of the Constitution wanted to make sure that the people's rights would always be safe and that the central or federal government would never become too powerful. A government ought to have three major powers: to make laws, to carry out those laws, and to provide justice under law for the best interests of the people. Should these three functions be in the hands of one person or one group, there would be great danger that that person or group could use the power for personal profit rather than for the people. To guard against this possibility, the Constitution provided for three major branches of government: the legislature, or congress, to make laws; the executive to carry out the laws; and the judiciary to watch over the rights of the people as described in the Constitution.

The powers of these three branches of the government are described carefully in the Constitution. To make sure that the government should never take more power than it was granted in the Constitution, it was carefully stated that any power not given to the government should forever belong to the states. Another reason for describing carefully the powers of the three branches was to prevent any one branch from becoming stronger than the others. Each job in the running of the country was balanced between the legislative, the executive and the judicial branches. Each part of the government can only function in relation to the others. This system not only balances power between the three branches, but also provides a check on each branch by the others. A good example of the check system can be found in the manner in which laws become laws. The legislature, or Congress, has the job of drafting laws for the country. Once a bill[1] has been passed by the two houses, the Senate and the House of Representatives, the Congress must send a copy to the chief executive, the president of the United States, for his approval. He then has several options as to what he may do. For instance, he may agree with the bill and sign the copy, in which case the law goes into effect. Or, if he should feel that it is not a good law, he may veto it. Vetoing means that he refuses to sign. Should he do that, the copy is returned to the house of Congress in which it originated. If the Congress, sure that the proposed law is a necessary one, passes it again by a two-thirds majority, the bill becomes a law regardless of the president's veto. The people are represented in Congress, and if they still favor the law, it is more democratic that they should have it.

The checks system goes further. The judicial branch has its say about the laws of the land. Once the Congress and the president have agreed upon a law, it must be enforced all over the United States. If someone disagrees with a federal law and challenges it by disobeying it, the case is brought into the court system of the United States. If the Supreme Court decides to hear the case, it has the duty of examining the law and determining if it is constitutional, or in other words, whether the law is in keeping with the rights of the people as outlined in the Constitution.

This system of balanced power and of checks between the branches of the government means that at all times the people's rights and interests are being carefully guarded. It must be stressed, however, that as Thomas Jefferson[2] said "Eternal vigilance is the price of liberty," and if the people of the United States, their elected representatives, and their judges are not constantly vigilant, no mere words on paper are going to protect their freedom.

[1] A bill is the name given to a law before it is signed by the president.

[2] Thomas Jefferson was the principal writer of the Declaration of Independence and the third president of the United States.

Fact-Finding Exercise

Read the passage once. Then read the following statements. Scan the article quickly to find out if each statement is true (T) or false (F). If a statement is false, change it so that it is true.

1. ____ T ____ F   The United States became independent in 1775.

   _____

2. ____ T ____ F   The first U.S. government did not have a president.

   _____

3. ____ T ____ F   The United States' present government began in 1787.

   _____

4. ____ T ____ F   The U.S. Constitution described two branches of the government: the legislative and the judicial.

   _____

5. ___ T ___ F   The system of checks and balances prevents one branch of government from becoming too powerful.

_____

6. ___ T ___ F   If the president disagrees with a new bill, it can never become a law.

_____

Read each question carefully. Circle the number or letter of the correct answer, or write your answer in the space provided.

1. Read lines 4–6. What does **at that point** mean?
    a. 1775
    b. 1787
    c. Between 1775 and 1787

2. Read lines 6–10.
    a. What was the men's **cause?**

    _____

    b. In line 8, what does **that Congress** refer to ?

    _____

3. Read lines 10–11.
    a. **Initial** means
        1. a letter of the alphabet
        2. the first
        3. the most difficult
    b. **Rule** means
        1. law
        2. state
        3. colony
    c. This sentence means that the people wanted to
        1. start new governments instead of the colonial government
        2. establish the colonial government again
        3. get rid of all forms of government

4. Read lines 14–16. "The Continental Congress was without legal foundation ..." This sentence means that
    a. the Continental Congress broke the law
    b. the Continental Congress did not make laws
    c. the Continental Congress had no legal authority

5. Read lines 16–21.

   a. In line 17, **reluctantly** means
      1. recently
      2. unanimously
      3. unwillingly

   b. Complete the following sentence:

      Gary wanted to find a job in New York because he thinks it is an exciting city. When he was unable to find a job there, he reluctantly
      1. accepted a job in New Jersey
      2. continued looking for a job

   c. In line 17, **majority** means
      1. some of the people
      2. more than half of the people
      3. all of the people

   d. In line 20, **therefore** means
      1. furthermore
      2. in addition
      3. as a result

6. Read lines 22–24. **Whose** refers to
   a. the president
   b. the chairman
   c. the Congress

7. Read lines 25–28. What types of control was the Congress not given?

   _____

   _____

   _____

8. Read lines 29–34.

   a. In lines 31–32, **discontent** means
      1. discomfort
      2. dissatisfaction
      3. disagreement

   b. Why were the people discontented?

      _____

9. Read lines 42–44. **Pioneers** are people who
   a. create new systems of government
   b. set things up based on what they do not want
   c. do something that no one has ever done before

10. Read lines 53–57.
    a. What is a **dilemma?**
       1. It is a problem with two possible good solutions.
       2. It is a problem with two difficulties and one good solution.
       3. It is a problem with two possible solutions, neither of which is perfect.
    b. What follows **on the one hand** and **on the other hand?**
       1. The two possible solutions to the problem
       2. Two good solutions to the problem
       3. Two bad solutions to the problem
    c. What is **the heart and soul of the Constitution?**

    _____

11. Read lines 62–64. What are **hands?**
    a. Law
    b. Control
    c. Body parts

12. Read lines 80–85.
    a. What is a **bill?**

    _____

    b. How do you know?

    _____

    c. This type of information is called a

    _____

13. Read lines 85–86.

    a. What does **veto** mean?

    _____

    b. In line 89, **regardless of** means

       1. in addition to
       2. because of
       3. in spite of

    c. Complete the following sentence:

    Thomas wanted to go to the beach with his friends. He heard on the radio that it might rain in the afternoon. He decided to go to the beach regardless of

       1. the weather report
       2. his friends

14. Read lines 101–104.

    a. Who was Thomas Jefferson?

    _____

    b. Where did you find this information?

    _____

C.   Word Forms

Part 1

In English, verbs can change to nouns in several ways. Some verbs become nouns by adding the suffix *-ment,* for example, *equip (v.), equipment (n.)*
Complete each sentence with the correct form of the words on the left. **Use the correct tense of the verbs, in either the affirmative or the negative form. Use the singular or plural form of the nouns.**

establish *(v.)*
establishment *(n.)*

1. a. Next year, the university _____ a new scholarship fund for foreign students.
    b. The permanent _____ of this type of scholarship fund will enable more students to study in this country.

agree *(v.)*
agreement *(n.)*

2. a. Tony _____ with us about going to the movies last night. In fact, we had an argument about it.
    b. We finally reached a mutual _____ after we found a movie that Tony really wanted to see.

replace *(v.)*
replacement *(n.)*

3. a. When my car broke down, I took it to the mechanic, who said that the carburetor needed _____.
    b. He not only _____ the carburetor, but he also tuned up the engine, and it cost me $800!

pay *(v.)*
payment *(n.)*

4. a. At registration, Phoebe _____ the full cost of her tuition at once.
    b. She arranged to cover her tuition in several _____ over four months.

enforce *(v.)*
enforcement *(n.)*

5. a. Rebecca is doing a study on law _____ for her master's thesis.
    b. She has discovered that some police precincts _____ the law as effectively as other precincts do.

In English, some adjectives become nouns by deleting the final -t and adding -ce, for example, *competent (adj.), competence (n.).*

Complete each sentence with the correct form of the words on the left. **Use the singular form of the nouns.**

reluctant *(adj.)*
reluctance *(n.)*

1. a. Charles felt quite _____ about driving alone from New York to Chicago to attend a conference. We all understood his unwillingness to travel so far by himself.
   b. Because of his _____ to drive alone, he decided to take the train instead.

vigilant *(adj.)*
vigilance *(n.)*

2. a. It has rained so little in California for the last six years that forest rangers need to be especially _____ in watching for forest fires.
   b. Unfortunately, in spite of their around-the-clock _____, fires have started and gotten out of control, causing the loss of thousands of acres of forest.

resistant *(adj.)*
resistance *(n.)*

3. a. My grandparents are quite _____ to any kind of change.
   b. Sometimes their _____ is humorous. For example, they refuse to buy a new car, even though theirs is 30 years old and always breaks down when they drive into town. When the phone rings on Saturday morning, we always know who it is.

distant *(adj.)*
distance *(n.)*

4. a. Julie called her parents long _____ last night.
   b. Unfortunately, the connection was very poor; their voices sounded so _____ that Julie hung up and tried the call again.

D. DICTIONARY SKILLS

Read the dictionary entry for each word. Indicate the number of the definition and write the synonym or meaning in the space provided. Remember that you may need to change the wording of the definition in order to have a grammatically correct sentence.

1.

> **cause** *n* **1 a** a reason for an action or condition: motive **b** something that brings about an effect or a result **c** a person or thing that is the occasion of an action or state; *esp:* an agent that brings something about **2 a** a ground for legal action **b** Case **3** a matter or question to be decided **4** a principle or movement militantly defended or supported

The Continental Congress was made up of men who believed in independence and who believed very strongly in the
(____)_____ that they supported.

2.

> **assembly** *n pl* **-blies 1** a company of persons gathered for deliberation and legislation, worship, or entertainment **2** a legislative body; *specif:* the lower house of a legislature **3** assemblage 1, 2 **4** a signal for troops to assemble or fall in **5** the fitting together of manufactured parts into a complete machine, structure, or unit of a machine **b** a collection of parts so assembled

The thirteen new states had elected governors and representative
(____)_____.

3.

> **erase** *vb* **erased; eras-ing 1 a** to rub or scrape out (as written, painted, or engraved letters) **b** to remove (recorded matter) from a magnetic tape or wire **c** to delete from a computer storage device **2 a** to remove from existence or memory as if by erasing **b** to nullify the effect or force of

It would have been impossible to (____)_____
the individual states.

4.

> **check** *n* **1 a** a sudden stoppage of a forward course or progress: arrest **b** a checking of an opposing player (as in ice hockey)
> **2** a sudden pause or break in a progression
> **3** one that arrests, limits, or restrains: restraint **4 a** a standard for testing and evaluation: criterion **b** examination
> **c** inspection, investigation **5** a written order directing a bank to pay money as instructed

This system of government provides a (＿)＿＿＿＿＿＿＿＿＿＿
on each branch by the other two.

Read the article a second time. Underline what you think are the main ideas. Then scan the article and complete the following outline, using the sentences that you have underlined to help you. You will use this outline later to answer specific questions about the article.

I. The Origin of the Federal System of Government

    A.

    B. The Continental Congress existed, but had no legal power

    C. Legal governments in the states were established to replace colonial rule

    D.

II.

    A. Its purpose:

    B. The feelings of the writers of the Constitution:

        1.

        2. They did not want a strong central government

        3.

        4.

III.

    A. The purpose of this system:

        1.

        2.

        3.

    B. The powers not given to the government belong to the states

    C.

IV.

    A. The legislature, or Congress, drafts a law

    B.

    C.

        1.

        2.

    D. If someone challenges the law, the judicial branch determines whether the law is constitutional or not

Information Organization Quiz and Summary

Read each question carefully. Use your notes to answer the questions. Do not refer back to the text. Write your answers in the space provided under each question. When you are finished, write a brief summary of the article.

1. a. What kind of government did the United States have before the Constitution was written?

    _____

    _____

    b. Was this government successful? Why, or why not?

    _____

    _____

2. What features of government didn't the writers of the Constitution want?

    _____

    _____

3. a. What is the purpose of the system of checks and balances?

    _____

    _____

    b. How does it work?

    _____

    _____

    _____

4. How are laws made in the United States?

    _____

    _____

Summary

_____

_____

_____

_____

_____

G. *Critical Thinking Strategies*

Read each question carefully. Write your response in the space provided. Remember that there is no one correct answer. Your response depends on what **you** think.

1. Read the first paragraph. Why does the article begin with a series of questions? In other words, what do you think is the author's purpose in asking the reader questions at the beginning of the reading passage?

_____

_____

_____

_____

2. Read lines 44–48. Why do you think these people were so sure about what kind of government they did *not* want?

_____

_____

_____

_____

3. Read the description of the system of checks and balances in lines 58–98. Do you think that this system adequately protects the people's rights and that it prevents the federal government from becoming too powerful? Explain your answer.

_____

_____

_____

_____

4. Read lines 60–62: "A government ought to have three major powers: to make laws, to carry out those laws, and to provide justice under law for the best interests of the people." Do you agree or disagree with this statement? That is, do you think these should be the major powers of any government? Explain your answer.

_____

_____

_____

_____

5. After reading this selection, specifically lines 16–19, 45–49, and 70–72, what can you understand about the individuality of the states in the United States? For instance, how do you think that the fact that the United States is divided into states affects American culture and the attitudes of the people in each state?

_____

_____

_____

_____

H. *Follow-up Discussion* AND *Writing Activities*

1. **Jigsaw Reading:** You are going to read about the three branches of the U.S. government: the legislative branch, the executive branch, and the judicial branch.

   a. First, read the paragraph entitled *The System of Checks and Balances* below. Discuss it in class to make sure everyone understands it.

   b. Second, work in a group of three or four students. Each group will read about one branch of government on the following pages. Group A will read about the legislative branch, Group B will read about the executive branch, and Group C will read about the judicial branch. If your class is large, then you may have more than one Group A, B, or C; just make sure that at least one group reads about each branch of the government. After reading the paragraph, discuss it to make sure everyone in the group understands about their particular branch.

   c. Third, set up different groups so that each group has a student or students who have read about the three different branches. In these new groups, tell each other what you have read about each branch. Take notes about the other two readings. Do not look back at your readings. Ask each other questions to make sure that all the students in your group understand how the three branches work.

   d. Finally, work together to complete the Federal System of Government Chart on page 153. When your group is finished, compare your chart with the other groups' charts.

The System of Checks and Balances

The writers of the Constitution wanted to make sure that the people's rights would always be safe and that the federal government would never become too powerful. Therefore, the writers of the Constitution set up three branches of government: the legislature, or Congress, to make laws; the executive branch—the president—to carry out the laws; the judicial branch, to watch over the rights of the people. The system of checks and balances makes sure that one branch cannot become stronger than another. This system not only balances power among the three branches but also provides a check on each branch by the others.

Group A Only: *The Legislative Branch*

The legislative branch, or Congress, represents all states fairly. It consists of two parts: the House of Representatives and the Senate. The vice president of the United States acts as the president of the Senate. Each state has two senators, who are elected every six years. The number of members in the House of Representatives depends on the population of each state. Representatives are elected every two years. To be elected as a senator, a person must be at least 30 years old, have been a citizen for nine years, and be a resident of the state s/he will represent. To be elected as a representative, a person must be at least 25 years old, have been a citizen for seven years, and be a resident of the state s/he will represent.

The major job of the Congress is to make laws. If the president vetoes, or rejects, a proposed law, the Congress can pass the law anyway by getting a two-thirds majority vote. Congress can also declare war by getting a two-thirds majority vote of the senators and representatives. The House of Representatives can also impeach the president. This means that the House can charge the president with a crime. In this case, the Senate will put the president on trial, so the vice president must resign as the president of the Senate. The Senate votes to approve the justices that the president appoints to the Supreme Court. These are just a few of the legislative branch's many responsibilities.

Group B's Information:

_____

_____

_____

_____

_____

_____

_____

Group C's Information:

_____

_____

_____

_____

_____

_____

_____

Group B Only: *The Executive Branch*

The executive branch of the government puts the country's laws into effect. The president of the United States is a member of the executive branch. The president must be at least 35 years old and be a natural citizen of the United States. In addition, he must have lived in the United States for at least 14 years and be a civilian. The president is elected every four years and cannot serve more than two terms in a row. The vice president acts as president of the Senate. When the president receives a bill from Congress, he must sign it in order for it to become a law. However, if he disagrees with the law, he can veto, or reject, it. The president can also ask the Congress to declare war. He also appoints the justices to the Supreme Court. He must do his job according to the Constitution, or he may be impeached, that is, charged with a crime by Congress. The executive branch is a very important part of the U.S. government and must work with the other two branches according to the Constitution.

Group A's Information:

_____

_____

_____

_____

_____

_____

_____

_____

Group C's Information:

_____

_____

_____

_____

_____

_____

_____

_____

Group C Only: *The Judicial Branch*

The judicial branch of government is the system of courts in the United States. Its job is to enforce the laws. The Supreme Court is the highest court in the country. It consists of nine justices: one chief justice and eight associate justices. The Constitution does not state any specific requirements for Supreme Court positions. The president appoints the justices, but the Senate must approve them. The justices are appointed for life. The Supreme Court not only makes sure that people obey the laws but can also declare a law unconstitutional. In other words, the Supreme Court can decide if a law is not in agreement with the Constitution. Furthermore, the chief justice acts as president of the Senate if there is an impeachment trial. In an impeachment trial, the Congress charges the president of the United States with a crime. The judicial branch works together with the legislative and executive branches to protect the Constitution and the rights of the people.

Group A's Information:

_____
_____
_____
_____
_____
_____
_____

Group B's Information:

_____
_____
_____
_____
_____
_____
_____

The Federal System of Government

2. In your groups, work together to complete the following chart. Do not look back to the paragraphs you have read.

	Legislative Branch	**Executive Branch**	**Judicial Branch**
Function			
Number of Members	Congress: _____ Senators _____ Representatives	1. 2. (acts as president of the Senate)	Justices: _____ Chief Justice _____ Associate Justices
Term of Office	Senate: House of Representatives:	President:	Justices:
Requirements	Senator: 1. 2. 3. 4. Representative: 1. 2.	President: 1. 2. 3. 4.	
Responsibilities: Laws	1. 2.	President: 1. 2. 3.	
Responsibilities: War		President:	
Impeachment	House of Representatives: Senate:	President: Vice President:	Chief Justice of the Supreme Court:

2. Alone, or with classmates from your country, write a description of the form of government in your country. Compare it with the form of government in the United States. For example, how are laws made? Who is the leader of the country? How is he or she granted this position? Compare your country's form of government with those of the other students' countries.

3. **Write in your journal.** Is there something that the writers of the Constitution overlooked in the system of checks and balances and that you think is important? In other words, did they forget to include a check or balance that you think is necessary to help control the federal government and keep it from becoming too powerful? Explain your answer.

 Surfing THE *INTERNET*

1. a. In class, list four or five of the possible forms of government. Divide the class into groups so that each group will research one of the forms of government you have listed.
   b. Use the Internet to research the form of government your group has chosen. Enter the form of government in your favorite search engine. Print out the information you find.
   c. In class, use your printouts to help you describe the form of government your group is researching. Create a chart comparable to the U.S. Government chart.
   d. In class, form groups with the other students so that each group contains at least one student who has studied each form of government. Discuss your charts, and compare the features of each form of government. Make sure that each member of the group understands the different forms of government.

2. Imagine that your group is a panel of experts. You have been selected as advisers to a newly established country to help establish a form of government that will be appropriate for that country and its people. Select one of the forms of government that your class has described, and present it to the representatives of the newly formed country. Give specific reasons why this particular form of government will be beneficial for the country. Discuss your decisions with your classmates.

Optional Activity: The writers of the Constitution realized that it might need to be modified over the years, so they allowed for amendments to be made. However, to insure that these changes could not be made easily or quickly, they made the amendment process very complex. Search the Internet to find out how an amendment to the Constitution is made. Describe the process. How does this procedure help insure that power ultimately rests with the individual states and not the federal government?

Cloze Quiz

Chapter 7: The Federal System of Government

Read the passage on this page. Fill in the blanks below with one word from the list. Use each word once.

afraid	easy	government	other	states
Constitution	endanger	hand	pioneers	strong
democratic	found	king	really	too
dilemma	freedoms	men	solution	undesirable

To create a government was not an _____ thing to do.
(1)

Remember that in 1787 the _____ at the convention in
(2)

Philadelphia were _____ in the setting up of a
(3)

_____ republican government. They _____ only
(4)   (5)

knew what they did not want. They did not want a _____, and
(6)

they did not want _____ strong a central government because
(7)

they were _____ of losing their own _____. They
(8)   (9)

certainly wanted to keep the _____ as they were.
(10)

Here was a _____. On the one _____, it
(11)   (12)

seemed that a _____ central government was very
(13)

_____ because it might _____ the people's liberties.
(14)   (15)

On the _____ hand, a weak central _____ had
(16)   (17)

proven inadequate. The _____ these men _____ is
(18)   (19)

called the system of checks and balances, and it is the heart and soul of the

_____.
(20)

Too Soon Old, Too Late Wise

by Evan Thomas with Adam Wolfberg

Newsweek

Prereading Preparation

1. Look at the photograph. Think about which one of these professors you would prefer to have as a teacher. Write down the reasons why you would choose one professor over the other. Compare your response with your classmates', and discuss whether the reasons people give are logical or emotional.

2. How old should a person be when he or she retires?

3. Should a person be required by law to retire at a certain age? Why, or why not?

4. In your country, must a person retire at a certain age? Why, or why not?

5. Work with a partner. Do you think there are some professions or jobs—e.g., police officers, airline pilots, etc.—from which people should retire at a specific age? Make a list of these jobs and the age at which people should retire from them. Discuss your list with your classmates.

The students of Prof. Paul Weiss at Catholic University of America had to be careful about where they sat in his classroom. Too far away from the podium and Professor Weiss, who is a bit hard of hearing, might not catch their questions. Too close and they risked getting an aimless whack from his cane. But over the years the students kept coming back because Weiss taught them to think. "He runs the class by throwing out a series of theses. Then he basically says, 'Attack me,'" recalls a former student, Father Robert Spitzer, 39, now a philosophy professor at Seattle University.

Paul Weiss[1], 90, is a world-class philosopher, an emeritus Sterling Professor at Yale and author of a score of books. He was once regarded as a prize catch by Catholic U., a financially pinched school of modest reputation in Washington, D.C. But last summer Weiss was told that he was being demoted to teaching graduate students part time. The reason, according to the university, was "shifting priorities." Weiss's highly personal brand of metaphysics no longer suited the needs of the university's philosophy department.

But the real reason that Weiss was shoved aside, according to a report by the U.S. Equal Employment Opportunity Commission, was his age. When an EEOC investigator asked a university official what factors, other than his salary and 20-year employment, went into the decision not to renew his teaching contract, the official answered, "He's 90." Undergraduates should not be taught by someone like "a grandfather," the official told the EEOC; Weiss should make way "for a younger man." Earlier this month, the EEOC gave Catholic a year to work out a settlement with Weiss. If the university fails, the agency will sue for age discrimination.

When is a teacher too old to teach? Airline pilots start losing their reflexes as they age, and senility and infirmity can be incapacitating in any profession. But philosophers are supposed to just get wiser as they get older. Bertrand Russell worked into his 90s, Kant into his 70s, and Socrates until he was about 70 and the Athenian tenure committee chose not to renew his contract. Weiss believes he's another wise man handed a goblet of hemlock. Weiss is determined to get his job back, even if it means a messy lawsuit.

Indeed, Weiss can't wait to go to court. A gnarled little man who lurches about his book-filled apartment with the aid of two canes, the professor loves confrontation. A high-school dropout (his father was a tinsmith, his mother a maid), Weiss took boxing lessons before going to night school at City College of New York. In 1929 he took his Ph.D. at Harvard. . . . Teaching philosophy at Yale in the late '40s, Weiss was the first Jewish faculty member at Yale College. . . .

---

[1]Prof. Weiss died in 2002. This article was written before his death.

Not Modest: Father William Byron, Catholic's president, insists that the university went out of its way to care for Weiss. He says that Catholic allowed Weiss to teach students out of his apartment after he was slowed down by a back operation two years ago. Such an arrangement is "absolutely unprecedented," Father Byron told *The Washington Post*. "False!" cries Professor Weiss. "Wittgenstein had students come to his rooms at Cambridge," he declares. "Alfred Whitehead had students come to his rooms at Harvard. I know. I was one of them." Weiss is not modest about the company he keeps. He also compares himself to Plato ("who was out in left field, too"). In testifying before the EEOC, Catholic administrators alluded to Weiss's "fading reputation." "Reputation!" exclaims Weiss. "*They* have no reputation. I was in *Who's Who in the World*. They're not. They teach philosophy. I'm a philosopher."

Weiss admits that he has a poor memory. For a scholar, isn't that somewhat of a liability? "I've *always* had a bad memory," he snaps. "I'm not haunted by what I know. I think every issue afresh. A philosopher," he continues, "is an arrogant man who asks himself fresh questions." Weiss is delighted by the publicity his case has attracted. Columnist William F. Buckley Jr., who studied under Weiss at Yale, accused Catholic of "shabbily" treating a "truly eminent" man. But Weiss was mildly offended when *The Washington Post* described him as a "manic lizard." "What are they trying to convey by these references to reptiles?" he asks a visiting journalist, who doesn't quite have the heart to tell him that he looks like one. "That your movements are quick?" the visitor suggests. "Hmm," he ponders. "Makes sense." He raps his cane.

Weiss shows off his latest manuscript, "Being and Other Realities," 500 pages of typescript covered with changes in black ink. "Revise! Revise!" he growls. "I am constantly revising." He works on the book from morning until night but says he misses his students. "I cherish teaching," he says. "When will he be ready to give it up? "When I'm vague and puttering," he barks, in a tone that defies anyone to suggest that he is either.

Fact-Finding Exercise

Read the passage once. Then read the following statements. Scan the article quickly to find out if each statement is true (T) or false (F). If a statement is false, change it so that it is true.

1. ____ T ____ F   Prof. Paul Weiss teaches philosophy at Catholic University.

   _____

2. ____ T ____ F   Officials at Catholic University believe that Prof. Weiss is too old to teach.

   _____

3. ____ T ____ F   Prof. Paul Weiss wants to stop teaching because of his age.

   _____

4. ____ T ____ F   Prof. Weiss does not want to go to court to settle his problem with the university.

   _____

5. ____ T ____ F   Prof. Weiss studied at Yale College.

   _____

6. ____ T ____ F   This situation has attracted a lot of publicity.

   _____

Read each question carefully. Circle the number or letter of the correct answer, or write your answer in the space provided.

1. In lines 2–4, **a bit hard of hearing** means
   a. a little confusing
   b. a little difficult
   c. a little deaf

2. Read lines 6–7: "He **runs** the class by throwing out a series of theses." This sentence means
   a. he walks quickly in the class
   b. he asks the class
   c. he teaches the class

3. In lines 9–10, what is **a score of books?**
   a. Many books
   b. A few books
   c. A type of book

4. Read lines 12–13. What does **demoted** mean?
   a. Given a better job
   b. Given a less important job
   c. Given a new job

5. Read lines 13–14. Why is **"shifting priorities"** in quotation marks?
   a. To provide emphasis
   b. Because the author disagrees
   c. Because it is a direct quote

6. Read lines 16–20. What is the EEOC?

   _____

7. Read lines 20–22: "Weiss should make way 'for a younger man.'" This statement means that

    a. Weiss should let a younger man have his job
    b. Weiss should help younger students find jobs
    c. Weiss should give his office to a younger man

8. Read lines 25–26. **As they age** means

    a. as they reach a specific age
    b. as they get older
    c. as they work hard

9. Read lines 27–29.

    a. Who are the people referred to here?

    _____

    b. How do you know?

    _____

10. Read line 32: "Indeed, Weiss can't wait to go to court." This sentence means that

    a. Weiss wants to go to court
    b. Weiss doesn't want to go to court

11. Read lines 34–36. What is Prof. Weiss's family background?

    a. His parents were wealthy and well educated.
    b. His parents were wealthy but poorly educated.
    c. His parents were poor and poorly educated.
    d. His parents were poor but well educated.

12. Refer to lines 36–37. What is the purpose of the ellipses (…)?

    a. To show emphasis
    b. To indicate that text has been deleted
    c. to show direct speech

13. Read lines 38–45.

    a. **Unprecedented** describes something that
        1. happens all the time
        2. has never happened before
        3. is not permitted to happen

b. In line 45, who does **them** refer to?

_____

14. Read lines 46–49.
    a. Who does **they** refer to?

    _____

    b. Why is **they** in italics?

    _____

15. Read lines 50–51.
    a. What is a **liability?**
       1. An advantage
       2. A disadvantage
       3. A danger
    b. What might be a liability to a teacher?

    _____

C. Word Forms

Part 1

In English, some adjectives become nouns by adding the suffix *-ity*, for example, *real (adj.)*, *reality (n.)*.

Complete each sentence with the correct form of the words on the left.

equal *(adj.)*
equality *(n.)*

1. a. In the United States, the Constitution guarantees everyone _____ rights under the law.
    b. This guarantee of _____ was written over two hundred years ago.

infirm *(adj.)*
infirmity *(n.)*

2. a. Prof. Weiss does not consider his age to be an _____. He feels capable of teaching, even at 90.
    b. In other words, Prof. Weiss is 90 years old, but he is by no means _____.

public *(adj.)*
publicity *(n.)*

3. a. The lives of politicians and actors are always exposed to a lot of _____.
    b. However, some people do not always like having their private lives under _____ scrutiny, or examination.

senile *(adj.)*
senility *(n.)*

4. a. Contrary to popular myth, _____ is not an inevitable part of becoming older.
    b. In fact, most older people never become at all _____. Their minds remain sharp and clear.

anxious *(adj.)*
anxiety *(n.)*

5. a. Michael invariably experiences intense _____ right before taking an important exam.
    b. Because he tends to become so _____, he has begun doing special exercises to help him relax.

In English, some verbs become nouns by adding the suffix *-ance* or *-ence,* for example, *insist (v.), insistence (n.).*

Complete each sentence with the correct form of the words on the left. **Use the correct tense of the verbs in either the affirmative or the negative form. Use the singular or plural form of the nouns.**

defy *(v.)*
defiance *(n.)*

1. a. Eleanor _____ her parents' authority and stayed out until after midnight last Friday.
   b. Because of her open _____ of established rules, her parents grounded her for two weeks. In other words, she cannot go out on evenings or weekends for two weeks.

disturb *(v.)*
disturbance *(n.)*

2. a. Please _____ us for a few hours. I've just put the baby to sleep, and I need to take a nap, too.
   b. If you make any _____, she will wake up and begin to cry, and neither of us will get any rest.

insist *(v.)*
insistence *(n.)*

3. a. I don't understand your _____ on always eating dinner at home.
   b. Tonight, I absolutely _____ that we go out to a restaurant for dinner. It'll be my treat, too.

refer *(v.)*
reference *(n.)*

4. a. Gene didn't do well on his history paper because he _____ to any sources for his information.
   b. His history professor told him to rewrite the paper and to give several _____ in a bibliography.

insure *(v.)*
insurance *(n.)*

5. a. Connie made extra copies of her house keys and gave them to me as a sort of _____.
   b. If she loses them, she still _____ that she won't be locked out of her apartment.

D. DICTIONARY SKILLS

Choose the appropriate definition for each word. Then write the number and the synonym or meaning in the space provided. Remember that you may need to change the wording of the definition in order to have a grammatically correct sentence.

1.
> **messy** *adj* **1** marked by confusion, disorder, or dirt: untidy **2** lacking neatness or precision: careless, slovenly **3** extremely unpleasant or trying

Weiss is determined to get his job back, even if it means a(n)
(___)_____ lawsuit.

2.
> **declare** *v* **1** to make known formally or explicitly **2** to make evident: show **3** to state emphatically: affirm **4** to make a full statement of (one's taxable or dutiable property)

Prof. Weiss (___)_____ that Alfred North Whitehead had students come to his rooms at Harvard. He was one of those students.

3.
> **case** *n* **1 a** a set of circumstances or conditions **b** (1) a situation requiring investigation or action (as by the police) (2) the object of investigation or consideration **2** condition: *specif:* condition of body or mind **3** an inflectional form of a noun, pronoun, or adjective indicating its grammatical relation to other words **4 a** a suit or action in law or equity **b** the evidence supporting a conclusion or judgment **5** an instance of disease or injury

Prof. Weiss is delighted by the publicity his (___)_____ has attracted.

4.
> **vague** *adj* **1 a** not clearly expressed: stated in indefinite terms **b** not having a precise meaning **2 a** not clearly defined, grasped, or understood: indistinct **b** not clearly felt or sensed **3** not thinking or expressing one's thoughts clearly or precisely **4** not sharply outlined: hazy

Prof. Weiss said that he will give up teaching when he becomes a person who is (___)_____ .

Read the article a second time. Underline what you think are the main ideas. Then scan the article and complete the following flowchart, using the sentences that you have underlined to help you. You will use this flowchart later to answer specific questions about the article.

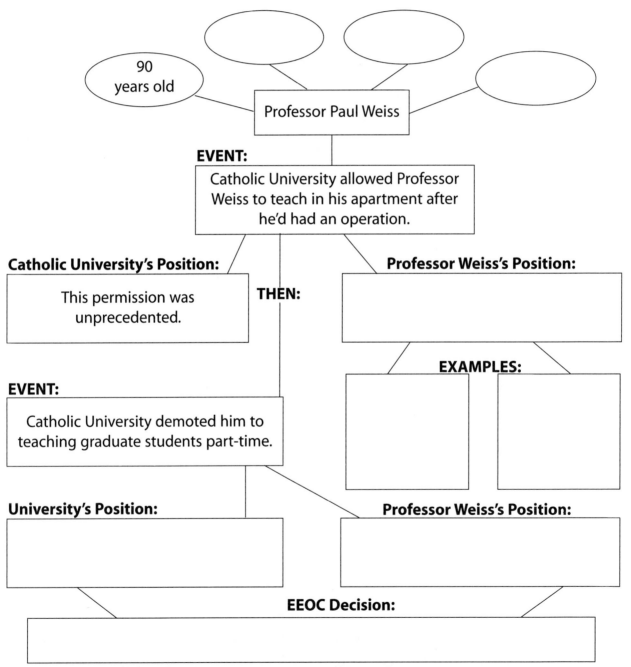

90 years old

Professor Paul Weiss

EVENT:
Catholic University allowed Professor Weiss to teach in his apartment after he'd had an operation.

Catholic University's Position:
This permission was unprecedented.

THEN:

Professor Weiss's Position:

EXAMPLES:

EVENT:
Catholic University demoted him to teaching graduate students part-time.

University's Position:

Professor Weiss's Position:

EEOC Decision:

Information Organization Quiz and Summary

Read each question carefully. Use your notes to answer the questions. Do not refer back to the text. Write your answers in the space provided under each question. When you are finished, write a brief summary of the article.

1. Describe Prof. Paul Weiss.

   _____

   _____

2. a. What did Catholic University do after Prof. Weiss had an operation?

      _____

      _____

   b. What did Catholic University say about this?

      _____

      _____

   c. What did Prof. Weiss say about this?

      _____

      _____

3. a. What did Catholic University do next?

      _____

      _____

   b. According to Catholic University, why did it do this?

      _____

      _____

   c. What does Prof. Weiss want to do about this situation?

      _____

      _____

4. What is the EEOC's decision about this situation?

_____

_____

_____

Summary

_____

_____

_____

_____

_____

G. *Critical Thinking Strategies*

Read each question carefully. Write your response in the space provided. Remember that there is no one correct answer. Your response depends on what **you** think.

1. Read lines 5–8. What do you think is Prof. Weiss's approach to teaching?

_____

_____

_____

_____

2. Read lines 38–49. How does this paragraph make clear that Prof. Weiss is not a modest man?

_____

_____

_____

_____

3. *Who's Who in the World* is a book that lists internationally notable people and gives a brief biography of each one. Read lines 48–49. Few teachers are listed in this book. What do you think this fact tells you about Prof. Weiss?

_____

_____

_____

_____

4. What do you think the author's opinion of Dr. Weiss's situation is? Does the author believe Dr. Weiss should be forced to retire? Why do you think so?

_____

_____

_____

_____

H. *Follow-up Discussion* AND *Writing Activities*

1. What type of person do you think Prof. Paul Weiss is? Describe the characteristics of Weiss's personality. For example, is he friendly? patient? intelligent? Write a composition and give example from the article for your description.

2. In your country, are there laws that require people to retire at a certain age? What are these laws? Do you agree with these laws? Why, or why not? Explain your answer.

3. In the United States, the Equal Employment Opportunity Commission (EEOC) does not allow employers to discriminate against older people. In other words, a person's age cannot be considered when an employer makes decisions about hiring, promoting, or firing employees. Do you agree with this policy? Why, or why not?

Cloze Quiz

Chapter 8: Too Soon Old, Too Late Wise

Read the passage on this page. Fill in the blanks below with one word from the list. Use each word once.

after	compares	insists	profession	unprecedented
age	determined	modest	students	until
allowed	even	operation	such	wait
care	infirmity	pilots	supposed	worked

When is a teacher too old to teach? Airline _____ start
(1)
losing their reflexes as they _____, and senility and
(2)
_____ can be incapacitating in any _____. But
(3)   (4)
philosophers are _____ to just get wiser as they get older.
(5)
Bertrand Russell _____ into his 90s, Kant into his 70s, and
(6)
Socrates _____ he was about 70. Weiss is _____ to
(7)   (8)
get his job back, _____ if it means a messy lawsuit.
(9)

Indeed, Weiss can't _____ to go to court. Father William
(10)
Byron, Catholic's president, _____ that the university went out
(11)
of its way to _____ for Weiss. He says that Catholic U.
(12)
_____ Weiss to teach students out of his apartment
(13)
_____ he was slowed down by a back _____ two
(14)   (15)
years ago. _____ an arrangement is "absolutely
(16)
_____," Father Byron told *The Washington Post*. "False!" cries
(17)
Professor Weiss. "Wittgenstein had _____ come to his rooms at
(18)
Cambridge," he declares. Weiss is not _____ about the company
(19)
he keeps. He also _____ himself to Plato.
(20)

The Pursuit of Excellence
by Jill Smolowe
Time

Prereading Preparation

1. In your country, what are the requirements for a student to attend college? Can any student go to college in your country? Why, or why not?

2. In the United States, what are the requirements for a foreign student to attend college? What are the requirements for an American student to attend college? Can any student go to college?

3. Why did you come to another country to study? Why do you think there are so many foreign students in American universities?

4. Take an in-class survey of the reasons students decide to study in another country.

   a. In small groups, discuss why students might choose to study abroad, e.g., cost, choice of subjects, etc.

   b. In your groups, list the reasons you decided to study abroad.

c. Compare your list with the other groups' lists. What is the most common reason students in your class have for studying abroad? The second most common reason? The third? Save your lists. Later, you will use these to compare to the responses from the survey you will do.

5. Look at the title of this article. What do you think it means?

The Pursuit of Excellence

1　　　Sometime around the seventh grade, many American students are
2　introduced to the tale of 10 blind men inspecting an elephant. When each blind
3　man reaches different conclusions about the creature, the students are invited to
4　consider whether truth is absolute or lies in the eye of the beholder. College
5　professors and administrators might want to remember that fable when they
6　take the measure of American higher education. Many of them, who tend to see
7　only what they stand to lose, perceive the beast as wounded, suffering from the
8　shocks of rising costs, dwindling resources and life-draining cutbacks. But
9　foreigners, who compare America's universities with their own, often reach very
10　different conclusions about the nature of the beast.

11　　　If sheer numbers provide any proof, America's universities and colleges are
12　the envy of the world. For all their abiding troubles, the United States' 3,500
13　institutions were flooded with 407,530 students from 193 different countries last
14　year. Asia led the way with 39,600 students from China and 36,610 from Japan,
15　followed by India and Canada. Many of the foreigners entered graduate and
16　undergraduate programs in roughly equal numbers. . . .

17　　　Most European and Asian universities provide an elite service to a small
18　and privileged clientele. While fully 60% of all U.S. high school graduates
19　attend college at some point in their life, just 30% of the comparable German
20　population, 28% of the French, 20% of the British and 37% of the Japanese
21　proceed beyond high school. German students who survive the *Abitur* or Britons
22　who pass their A levels may still not qualify for a top university at home, but
23　find American universities far more welcoming. Some U.S. schools acknowledge
24　the rigor of European secondary training and will give up to a year's credit to
25　foreigners who have passed their high school exams.

26　　　"The egalitarian conception that everyone has a right to an education
27　appropriate to his potential is a highly democratic and compassionate standard,"
28　says Marvin Bressler, professor of sociology and education specialist at
29　Princeton University. True, not all U.S. collegians can match the performance of
30　their foreign counterparts, but American institutions do offer students from rich
31　and poor families alike the chance to realize their full potential. "America
32　educates so many more people at university that one can't expect all those who

go to be either as well informed or intelligent as the much narrower band who go to English universities," says Briton Christopher Ricks, professor of English at Boston University. Having instructed at Cambridge, Rick knows that teaching T. S. Eliot to British undergraduates is an easier task. Yet he finds teaching at B.U. very rewarding. "I'm not against elitism," he says, "but I happen to like having people who are more eager to learn."

The democratic impulse to reach out to so many first took seed after World War II, when the G.I. bill made funding for higher education available to all returning soldiers. As universities expanded to handle the sudden influx, they developed the flexibility that has become one of the hallmarks of American higher learning. "In the U.S. there is a system of infinite chances," says Diane Ravitch, assistant secretary of education. "At 35, you can decide to go back to college, upgrade your education, change your profession."

While Americans take such flexibility for granted, foreigners do not. To French students, who are commonly expected at age 16 to select both a university and a specific course of study, the American practice of jumping not only from department to department but also from school to school seems a luxury. Japanese students find it all but impossible to transfer credits from one school to another. Thus students who initially enter a junior college and subsequently decide to earn a bachelor's degree must head overseas.

Many are attracted not only to the academic programs at a particular U.S. college but also to the larger community, which affords the chance to soak up the surrounding culture. Few foreign universities put much emphasis on the cozy communal life that characterizes American campuses from clubs and sports teams to student publications and theatrical societies. "The campus and the American university have become identical in people's minds," says Brown University President Vartan Gregorian. "In America it is assumed that a student's daily life is as important as his learning experience. . . ."

Foreign students also come in search of choices. America's menu of options—research universities, state institutions, private liberal-arts schools, community colleges, religious institutions, military academies—is unrivaled. "In Europe," says history professor Jonathan Steinberg, who has taught at both Harvard and Cambridge, "there is one system, and that is it." While students overseas usually must demonstrate expertise in a single field, whether law or philosophy or chemistry, most American universities insist that students sample natural and social sciences, languages and literature before choosing a field of concentration.

Such opposing philosophies grow out of different traditions and power structures. In Europe and Japan, universities are answerable only to a ministry of education, which sets academic standards and distributes money. While

73 centralization ensures that all students are equipped with roughly the same
74 resources and perform at roughly the same level, it also discourages
75 experimentation. "When they make mistakes, they make big ones," says Robert
76 Rosenzweig, president of the Association of American Universities. "They set a
77 system in wrong directions, and it's like steering a supertanker."

78 U.S. colleges, on the other hand, are so responsive to cultural currents that
79 they are often on the cutting edge of social change. Such sensitivity—some
80 might argue hypersensitivity—to the culture around them reflects the broad
81 array of constituencies to which college administrators must answer. The board
82 of trustees, composed of community and national leaders, serves as a referee
83 between the institutional culture and the surrounding community, alumni and
84 corporate donors who often earmark monies for specific expenditures, student
85 bodies that demand a voice in university life, legislators who apportion
86 government funds, and an often feisty faculty.

87 Smaller colleges are particularly attractive to foreign students because they
88 are likely to offer direct contact with professors. "We have one of the few
89 systems in the world where students are actually expected to go to class," says
90 Rosenzweig. With the exception of Britain, where much of the teaching takes
91 place in one-on-one tutorials, European students rarely come into direct contact
92 with professors until they reach graduate-level studies. Even lectures are
93 optional in Europe, since students are graded solely on examinations, with no
94 eye to class attendance or participation. . . .

95 In some respects, the independent spirit of the American university that
96 foreigners admire comes down to dollars and cents. All U.S. colleges, private and
97 public alike, must fight vigorously to stay alive. They compete not only for
98 students but also for faculty and research grants. Such competition, though
99 draining and distracting, can stimulate creativity and force administrators to
100 remain attentive to student needs. "U.S. students pay for their education," says
101 Ulrich Littmann, head of the German Fulbright Commission, "and demand a
102 commensurate value for what they—or their parents—pay."

103 Most universities abroad have state funding, but that luxury has a steep
104 price: universities have less opportunity to develop distinctive personalities and
105 define their own missions. . . . If the financial crisis besetting U.S. campuses is
106 mishandled, Americans may discover they don't know what they've got until
107 it's gone.

Fact-Finding Exercise

Read the passage once. Then read the following statements. Scan the article quickly to find out if each statement is true (T) or false (F). If a statement is false, change it so it is true.

1. _____ T _____ F   Most foreign students in American universities come from Canada.

_____

2. _____ T _____ F   Most U.S. high school graduates go to college.

_____

3. _____ T _____ F   Foreign students attend U.S. universities only for educational reasons.

_____

4. _____ T _____ F   Students in American universities must take a variety of courses in addition to courses in their major field.

_____

5. _____ T _____ F   In an American university, it is not likely that students will be in direct contact with their teachers.

_____

6. _____ T _____ F   Many American universities today are having financial problems.

_____

Read each question carefully. Circle the number or letter of the correct answer, or write your answer in the space provided.

1. Read the first paragraph. What do college professors and administrators believe about American universities?
   a. American universities are superior to foreign universities.
   b. There is a financial crisis in American universities.
   c. They think that American universities are very expensive.

2. Read lines 14–15. "Asia led the way with 39,600 students from China and 36,610 from Japan, followed by India and Canada." This statement means
   a. Asian students arrived first
   b. Chinese students were in front of Japanese students
   c. more students came from Asia than from anywhere else
   d. Indian students followed Japanese students

3. Read lines 15–16. This statement means
   a. half of foreign students entered undergraduate school and half entered graduate school
   b. more foreign students entered undergraduate school than graduate school

4. Read lines 17 and 18. Which word is a synonym of **elite?**

   _____

5. Read lines 18–21.
   a. **At some point in their life** means that most U.S. high school graduates
      1. enter college at the same age
      2. enter college before they get married
      3. enter college at different times

b. What is the **comparable German population?**
1. German high school graduates
2. German college students
3. German people

6. Read lines 21–23.
    a. What are the **Arbitur** and the **A levels?**

    _____

    b. How do you know?

    _____

7. Read lines 23–25.
    a. This statement means that
        1. European secondary training is more difficult than American secondary training
        2. American secondary training is more difficult than European secondary training
    b. **Secondary training** refers to
        1. graduate school
        2. college
        3. high school

8. Read lines 29–31.
    a. **Counterparts** refers to
        1. foreign college students
        2. American college students
        3. rich students
        4. poor students
    b. **Rich and poor families alike** means
        1. rich families are like poor families
        2. both rich families _and_ poor families
        3. rich families and poor families like each other

9. Read lines 43–45. **Chances** means

    a. risks
    b. opportunities
    c. accidents

10. Read lines 46–50. **Jumping from department to department** means

    a. taking gymnastics classes
    b. changing universities
    c. changing majors

11. Read lines 50–52.

    a. **all but impossible** means
       1. completely impossible
       2. almost impossible
       3. everything is impossible

    b. **Thus** means
       1. afterwards
       2. in addition
       3. as a result

    c. **Initially** means
       1. first
       2. second
       3. third

    d. **Subsequently** means
       1. first
       2. next
       3. last

12. Read lines 61–63.

    a. Which words are synonyms of **choices?**

    _____

    b. What is between the dashes (—)?
       1. New information about options
       2. Examples of options
       3. Contrasting information

13. Read lines 88–94.
    a. This statement means that students in European classes
       1. never attend classes
       2. must attend classes
       3. do not have to attend classes
    b. **Optional** means
       1. necessary
       2. not necessary
       3. important

14. Read lines 103–105. What follows the colon (:)?
    a. The cost of state funding
    b. An explanation of the price
    c. A description of universities

15. In lines 16, 60, and elsewhere there are ellipses (. . .) at the end of the paragraph. These dots indicate that
    a. the last sentence is incomplete
    b. text has been deleted from the article
    c. there are exactly three sentences missing

C. Word Forms

Part 1

In English, some adjectives become nouns by adding the suffix *-ity,* for example, *fatal (adj.), fatality (n.).*

Complete each sentence with the correct form of the words on the left. **Use the singular or plural form of the nouns.**

individual *(adj.)*
individuality *(n.)*

1. a. Even though they may be in a large class, students like to receive _____ treatment from their teachers.
    b. Everyone likes to preserve their _____ even if they are part of a large group.

creative *(adj.)*
creativity *(n.)*

2. a. People can demonstrate _____ in many ways.
    b. For instance, some people have _____ ways of expressing themselves in words, others in decorating their homes, still others in painting or photography.

diverse *(adj.)*
diversity *(n.)*

3. a. In a typical ESL classroom, you will find students from a wide _____ of countries.
    b. In fact, even if students are from the same country, they may come from _____ backgrounds.

national *(adj.)*
nationality *(n.)*

4. a. Each country has its own _____ anthem, or song.
    b. There are students of very different _____ in this class.

flexible *(adj.)*
flexibility *(n.)*

5. a. There is considerable _____ in this English program.
    b. For example, the days and the hours of classes are quite _____.

In English, some adjectives become nouns by deleting the final -t and adding -ce, for example, *negligent (adj.), negligence (n.).*

Complete each sentence with the correct form of the words on the left.

independent *(adj.)*
independence *(n.)*

1. a. In the past several years, many countries have struggled for and gained their _____.
   b. These newly _____ countries usually have to contend with many difficulties as they try to maintain stability.

different *(adj.)*
difference *(n.)*

2. a. I haven't noticed any _____ in the quality of the food in this restaurant since they hired a new cook last week.
   b. The meals don't taste any _____ than they did last week.

dominant *(adj.)*
dominance *(n.)*

3. a. According to geneticists, brown eyes are always _____ over blue eyes.
   b. This _____ means that if one parent has brown eyes and the other parent has blue eyes, the children will most likely have brown eyes.

excellent *(adj.)*
excellence *(n.)*

4. a. We all strive for _____, and sometimes we achieve it.
   b. Even if everything we do isn't always _____, we can always try harder the next time.

important *(adj.)*
importance *(n.)*

5. a. The students want to know how much _____ the teacher is going to give to their homework.
   b. In other words, they want to know how _____ the homework is to their grade.

D. DICTIONARY SKILLS

Choose the appropriate definition for each word. Then write the number and the synonym or meaning in the space provided. Remember that you may need to change the wording of the definition in order to have a grammatically correct sentence.

1.
> **roughly** *adv* **1** in a rough manner: as **a** with harshness or violence **b** in crude fashion: imperfectly **2** without completeness or exactness: approximately

Many of the foreigners entered graduate and undergraduate programs in (___)_____ equal numbers.

2.
> **match** *v* **1 a** to set in competition or opposition **b** to set in comparison **2** to join or give in marriage **3 a** to cause to correspond: suit **b** to be the counterpart of; *also,* to compare favorably with **4** to fit together or make suitable for fitting together

Not all U.S. collegians can (___)_____ the performance of their foreign counterparts.

3.
> **practice** *n* **1 a** actual performance or application **b** a repeated or customary action **c** the usual way of doing something **d** the form, manner, and order of conducting legal suits and prosecutions **2 a** a systematic exercise for proficiency **b** the condition of being proficient through systematic exercise **3** the continuous exercise of a profession

The American (___)_____ of jumping from department to department seems a luxury.

4.
> **demonstrate** *v* **1** to show clearly **2 a** to prove or make clear by reasoning or evidence **b** to illustrate and explain esp. with many examples **3** to show or prove the value or efficiency of to a prospective buyer

Students overseas must (___)_____ expertise in a single field, whether law or philosophy or chemistry.

Information Organization

Read the article a second time. Underline what you think are the main ideas. Then scan the article and complete the following chart, using the sentences that you have underlined to help you. You will use this chart later to answer specific questions about the article. Not all the boxes will be filled in.

	United States	Japan	Europe
Percent of high school graduates who attend college			
Differences between universities (freedom of choice)	1. 2. 3.	1.	France: 1.
Differences in types of colleges	1.		1.
Funding for education	1.	1.	1.

Information Organization Quiz and Summary

Read each question carefully. Use your notes to answer the questions. Do not refer back to the text. Write your answers in the space provided under each question. When you are finished, write a brief summary of the article.

1. a. What percent of U.S. high school graduates enter college?

    _____

    b. What percent of high school graduates enter college in countries in Europe and Asia?

    _____

    _____

2. What are some differences between universities in the United States and those in Europe and in Asia?

    _____

    _____

    _____

3. How are colleges in the United States different financially from colleges in other countries?

    _____

    _____

    _____

Summary

_____

_____

_____

_____

G. Critical Thinking Strategies

Read each question carefully. Write your response in the space provided. Remember that there is no one correct answer. Your response depends on what **you** think.

1. In lines 58–60, Brown University President Gregorian says, "In America it is assumed that a student's daily life is as important as his learning experience." From this statement, what expectations, other than academic, can we assume that American universities have of all their students, including foreign students?

   _____

   _____

   _____

   _____

2. Read lines 65–69. Why do you think American universities have these requirements?

   _____

   _____

   _____

   _____

3. In lines 95–102, the author discusses the money factor. What connection does she make between paying for one's education and the university's responsibility to its students?

   _____

   _____

   _____

   _____

4. Read lines 103–105. What do you think the author believes is the effect of state funding on foreign universities?

_____

_____

_____

_____

5. Think about how the author presented the information in this article.

a. Do you think she was objective or subjective in describing the American university system? Why do you think so? Refer to specific sentences in the reading to support your opinion.

_____

_____

_____

b. Do you think she was objective or subjective in describing foreign students? Why do you think so? Refer to specific sentences in the reading to support your opinion.

_____

_____

_____

_____

H. *Follow-up Discussion* AND *Writing Activities*

1. Refer back to the chart in Exercise E. Choose two differences between American universities and foreign universities. Using the following chart, write the differences you have chosen and list what you think the advantages and disadvantages are. Compare your chart with your classmates' charts.

	In the United States	In Japan	In Europe
Difference			
Advantages			
Disadvantages			
Difference			
Advantages			
Disadvantages			

2. a. Refer to the College Survey below. The purpose of this questionnaire is to collect data regarding students' reasons for studying in a foreign country. As a class, add more reasons to #5 in order to complete the survey.

    b. After you have finished the questionnaire, go outside your class alone or in pairs. Survey two or three international students. Then bring back your data and combine it with the other students' information. How do your results compare with the results you obtained in your class? Do you think that international students have similar reasons for studying in another country? What are the main reasons you discovered, in both your in-class and your out-of-class surveys?

College Survey		
1	**2**	**3**
Informant's Sex (M/F)		
1. What country are you from?		
2. What field do you plan to major in?		
3. Are you going to enter an undergraduate program or a graduate program?		
4. Why did you choose to study in the United States? Please indicate all the reasons that apply to you. • the cost of education • to study my major • the choice of courses • to improve my English • to get away from home • to learn about another country • other reasons (please specify)		
5. Read the reasons you have indicated for studying in the United States. Put them in order of importance. That is, write **1** next to your most important reason, **2** next to your second most important reason, etc.		

3. Describe your experience as a foreign student in the United States, or the experience of someone you know who has studied in the United States. What was positive about the experience? What was negative about the experience? Explain.

4. Work with one or two partners. List the potential difficulties of being a foreign student in the United States. Discuss how you can deal with these problems to reduce or eliminate them.

5. One problem that foreign students frequently encounter is loneliness and difficulty making friends. Work with a partner. Plan several strategies for reducing loneliness and making friends.

6. **Write in your journal.** Imagine that a friend wants to come to the United States to study. Write your friend a letter. Tell him or her what to expect as a foreign student and how to prepare before leaving home.

Cloze Quiz

Chapter 9: The Pursuit of Excellence

Read the passage on this page. Fill in the blanks below with one word from the list. Use each word once.

attracted	countries	expected	foreigners	provide
campuses	emphasis	flexibility	impossible	students
colleges	envy	flooded	initially	troubles
community	equal	followed	practice	undergraduate

If sheer numbers _____ any proof, America's universities and
_____ are the _____ of the world. For all their
(2)   (3)
abiding _____, the United States' 3,500 institutions were
(4)
_____ with 407,530 students from 193 different
(5)
_____ last year. Asia led the way with 39,600 _____
(6)
from China and 36,610 from Japan, _____ by India and Canada.
(8)
Many of the _____ entered graduate and _____
(9)
programs in roughly _____ numbers.   (10)
(11)
   Americans take academic _____ for granted, but foreigners
(12)
do not. To French students, who are commonly _____ at age 16
(13)
to select both a university and a specific course of study, the American
_____ of jumping not only from department to department but
(14)
also from school to school seems a luxury. Japanese students find it all but
_____ to transfer credits from one school to another. Thus
(15)
students who _____ enter a junior college and subsequently
(16)
decide to earn a bachelor's degree must head overseas.

Many are _____ not only to the academic programs at a
                    (17)
particular U.S. college but also to the larger _____, which affords
                                                              (18)
the chance to soak up the surrounding culture. Few foreign universities put

much _____ on the cozy communal life that characterizes
              (19)
American _____: from clubs and sports teams to student
                      (20)
publications and theatrical societies.

Unit 3 Review

J. Crossword Puzzle

Read the clues on the next page. Write the answers in the correct spaces in the puzzle.

Crossword Clues

Across

3. Sue will _____ you on the phone tonight.

5. A _____ consists of more than half (at least 51%) of a group.

9. International students must _____ their English proficiency before being admitted to an American college or university.

11. I _____ speak English well.

13. Susan was _____ from Manager to Assistant Manager because she was not doing a good job.

14. Each; every

15. The Congress is called the _____ branch because its purpose is to make laws.

18. _____ are very important things, listed in their order of importance.

19. The mayor made a _____ statement at the news conference.

20. The past tense of **do**

22. A _____ is one possible form of government.

23. When something is _____, it is a choice; it is not necessary.

Down

1. The system of checks and _____ ensures that no one in government has too much power.

2. A problem with no perfect solution

4. Opposite of **first**

6. Something which happens that has never happened before is an _____ event.

7. John was very _____ in describing the accident. He wasn't thinking clearly at the time.

8. High quality; superiority

10. Opposite of **beginning**

12. The opposite of **yes**

16. In the United States, the _____ of moving from one job to another is fairly common. In other countries, it is rare.

17. People must always be _____, or alert, in order to protect their rights.

21. I _____; he has

K. UNIT 3 DISCUSSION

1. In some countries, the government pays all educational costs for students. In other countries, it is the responsibility of each family. Each system has its advantages and disadvantages. Who do you think should cover the costs of education? In your response, discuss the advantages and disadvantages of both systems.

2. In some countries, the government sets up rules and guidelines that affect people's lives in many areas, e.g., family size, education, employment, retirement. Work in a small group. Choose one of these areas, or another area of your choice. The government has chosen your committee to set up guidelines for this area. In your group, make a list of rules. Present your rules to the class, and give reasons for your decisions.

1. A few years ago, many Americans in their 50s and 60s planned to retire early, but the economy weakened, decreasing people's savings. Thus, they no longer had the option to retire early. Would you feel anxious if this situation happened to you? What plans have you made for retirement? Do you look forward to it?

2. Read the following true-false questions and watch the video once or twice. Then answer the questions.

   a. ____ T ____ F   Michael and Roberta Brenner had enough assets to retire three years before they were interviewed.

   b. ____ T ____ F   According to the expert from Boston College, the typical 401(k) retirement account contains $100 thousand.

   c. ____ T ____ F   Fewer than 40 percent of Americans over 65 are working full or part-time.

   d. ____ T ____ F   The man who invented the 401(k), a type of retirement account, is not planning to retire soon.

   e. ____ T ____ F   The Brenners feel that working longer than they had planned may be a blessing in disguise.

3. The inventor of the 401(k) says people need a "very large nest egg" to live for 20 or 30 years in retirement. What is a nest egg? How much would you have to save to finance a comfortable retirement? When would you have to begin to save? Do you think governments should provide a comfortable retirement for all citizens? Is it possible for them to do so?

Thousands of students come to the United States to study every year. Using InfoTrac, type in "foreign students and the United States" and "United States and foreign universities" and find articles about where these students come from. Read two or three. Which countries send the most students to the United States? List the top five. Why do international students want to study here? What are the most popular majors among these students? Write a short report about your findings. Did any of the information you found surprise you? If so, what was it? Explain. Share your information with other students.

UNIT 4

SCIENCE AND TECHNOLOGY

10

Antarctica: Whose Continent Is It Anyway?
by Daniel and Sally Grotta
Popular Science

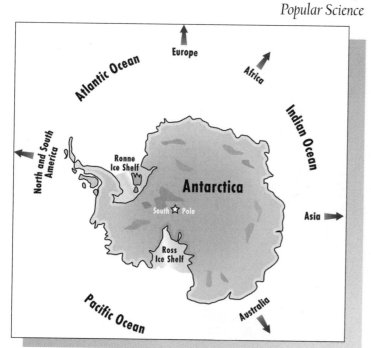

Prereading Preparation

1. Where is **Antarctica?**

2. Work with a partner. Discuss what you know about Antarctica, and fill in the chart below with your information.

Climate	Geography	People	Animals	Plants

3. Some scientists want to study Antarctica. What are some reasons why?

4. Look at the title. What do you think this article will discuss?

Antarctica: Whose Continent Is It Anyway?

Last February the *World Discoverer*, our cruise ship, stopped in front of a white ice cliff higher than the ship's mast. As large as France, the Ross Ice Shelf of Antarctica extends unbroken along the Ross Sea for hundreds of miles.

Like other passengers on our cruise ship, we had been lured by an irresistible attraction: the chance to visit the most remote place on Earth, and the most unusual. The coldest place on Earth is also the subject of conflicting interests: scientists, tourists, environmentalists, oil and mineral seekers.

Scientists treasure the unparalleled advantages for research; tourists prize the chance to visit Earth's last frontier; environmentalists fear that increases in both activities will pollute the continent and jeopardize its fabulous creatures; others contend that preserving Antarctica as a kind of world park will deprive the rest of the world of much needed oil and mineral reserves.

Fears of Antarctica's ruin through commercial exploitation have been partly reduced by the October, 1991, 31-nation signing of the Madrid Protocol, which bans oil and gas exploration for the next 50 years. But Antarctica's unique attributes—it is the coldest, driest, and highest continent—will keep it at the focus of conflicting scientific and touristic interests.

Think of a place as remote as the far side of the moon, as strange as Saturn and as inhospitable as Mars, and that will give some idea of what Antarctica is like. A mere 2.4 percent of its 5.4 million-square-mile land mass is ice-free, and, then, only for a few months a year. Scientists estimate that 70 percent of the world's fresh water is locked away in Antarctica's icecap; if it were ever to melt, sea levels might rise 200 feet. In Antarctica, winds can blow at better than 200 mph, and temperatures drop as low as minus 128.6°F. There's not a single village or town, not a tree, bush, or blade of grass on the entire continent.

But far from being merely a useless continent, Antarctica is vital to life on Earth. The continent's vast ice fields reflect sunlight back into space, preventing the planet from overheating. The cold water that the breakaway icebergs generate flows north and mixes with equatorial warm water, producing currents, clouds, and ultimately creating complex weather patterns. Antarctic seas teem with life, making them an important link in the world food chain. The frigid waters of the Southern Ocean are home to species of birds and mammals that are found nowhere else.

The National Science Foundation (NSF) is the government agency responsible for the U.S. stations in Antarctica. Because of the continent's extreme cold and almost complete isolation, the NSF considers it to be the best place to study and understand such phenomena as temperature circulation in the oceans, unique animal life, ozone depletion, and glacial history. And buried deep in layers of Antarctic ice lie clues to ancient climates, clues such as trapped

40　bubbles of atmospheric gases, which can help predict whether present and
41　future global warming poses a real threat.

42　　　Until scientists began the first serious study of the continent during the
43　1957–58 International Geophysical Year (IGY), a multicountry cooperative
44　research project, Antarctica was dismissed as a vast, useless continent.

45　　　Based upon early explorations and questionable land grants, seven
46　countries, including Great Britain, Chile, and Argentina, claim sovereignty over
47　vast tracts of the continent. However, as IGY wound down, the question of who
48　owns Antarctica came to a head. The 12 participating countries reached an
49　international agreement, the Antarctic Treaty, which took effect in June 1961.
50　The number has since grown, making 39 in all. It established Antarctica as a
51　"continent for science and peace," and temporarily set aside all claims of
52　sovereignty for as long as the treaty remains in effect.

53　　　The rules of the treaty meant that as tourists to Antarctica, passengers on
54　our cruise ship needed neither passports nor visas. Except for a handful of sites
55　of special scientific interest, specially protected areas, and specially managed
56　areas, there was nothing to restrict us from wandering anywhere we wanted.

57　　　Primarily because of its scientific and ecological importance, many
58　scientists feel that Antarctica should be dedicated to research only. They feel
59　that tourists should not be permitted to come. However, recent events have
60　shown that the greatest future threat to Antarctica may not be tourism or
61　scientific stations, but the worldwide thirst for oil and minerals. "The reason the
62　Antarctic Treaty was negotiated and went through so quickly," geologist John
63　Splettstoesser explains, "is that at the time, relatively few minerals were known
64　to exist there."

65　　　By the early 1970s, however, there were some indications that there might
66　be gas and oil in Antarctica. The treaty countries decided that no commercial
67　companies would be permitted to explore for resources. The Madrid Protocol
68　bans all exploration or commercial exploitation of natural resources on the
69　continent for the next 50 years.

70　　　Like the Antarctic Treaty itself, the Madrid Protocol is binding only on the 39
71　treaty countries. There's nothing to stop non-treaty countries from establishing
72　commercial bases anywhere on the continent and doing whatever they please.

73　　　Where do we go from here? So far, no non-treaty nation has expressed a
74　serious interest in setting up for business in Antarctica. So far, none of the
75　countries claiming sovereignty has moved to formally annex Antarctic territory.

76　　　So whose continent is Antarctica, anyway? [Former] Vice President Albert
77　Gore best expresses the feelings of those of us who have fallen in love with this
78　strange and spectacular land: "I think that it should be held in trust as a global
79　ecological reserve for all the people of the world, not just in this generation, but
80　later generations to come as well."

Fact-Finding Exercise

Read the passage once. Then read the following statements. Scan the article quickly to find out if each statement is true (T) or false (F). If a statement is false, change it so that it is true.

1. ____ T ____ F   Most people agree that Antarctica should be used for research.

_____

2. ____ T ____ F   Antarctica is the coldest place on earth.

_____

3. ____ T ____ F   Most of Antarctica is ice-free.

_____

4. ____ T ____ F   Antarctica is a useless continent.

_____

5. ____ T ____ F   Important information about the past may be buried under the Antarctic ice.

_____

6. ___ T ___ F   Thirty-nine countries have agreed to the Antarctic treaty.

_____

7. ___ T ___ F   Most tourists feel that Antarctica should be dedicated to scientific research only.

_____

8. ___ T ___ F   The Madrid Protocol allows countries to explore Antarctica for natural resources.

_____

Reading Analysis

Read each question carefully. Circle the number or letter of the correct answer, or write your answer in the space provided.

1. Read lines 1–2. What is the **World Discoverer**?

    _____

2. In line 1, who does **our** refer to?

    _____

3. Read lines 2–3. What is as large as France?
    a. The *World Discoverer*
    b. The Ross Ice Shelf
    c. Antarctica

4. a. In line 5, what follows the colon (**:**)?
        1. Additional information
        2. An example
        3. An explanation
    b. In line 5, what is an **irresistible attraction?**

        _____

        _____

5. Read lines 4–6: "We had been lured by an irresistible attraction: the chance to visit the most remote place on Earth." What does **lure** mean?
    a. Invite
    b. Visit
    c. Attract

6. In lines 6–7, what is the coldest place on Earth?

    _____

7. Read lines 8–12. In line 11, who does **others** refer to?

   a. Tourists
   b. Scientists
   c. Environmentalists
   d. Oil and mineral seekers

8. In lines 18–21, what does **a mere 2.4 percent** mean?

   a. Only 2.4 percent
   b. Exactly 2.4 percent
   c. Approximately 2.4 percent

9. Read lines 30–31. Which one of the following examples represents a **food chain?**

   a. Orange tree → oranges → people
   b. insects → birds → cats
   c. Farmer → supermarket → people

10. Read lines 42–44. What is **IGY?**

   _____

11. a. Read lines 42–44. When was Antarctica thought of as a useless continent?

      1. Before IGY
      2. After IGY

    b. When did scientists begin the first serious study of Antarctica?
      1. Before 1957
      2. 1957–1958
      3. After 1958

12. Read lines 47–48. "As IGY wound down, the question of who owns Antarctica came to a head." What does **came to a head** mean?

   a. Started a big argument
   b. Grew to a large size
   c. Became very important

13. In line 52, what does **sovereignty** mean?

   a Ownership
   b. Boundaries
   c. Continent

14. In line 54, what is **a handful?**
    a. A small number
    b. A large number

15. Read lines 54–56. Which word is a synonym for **sites?**

    _____

16. In lines 61–64, when does **at the time** refer to?

    _____

17. In line 71, what are **non-treaty countries?**

    _____

18. a. In lines 73–75, what does **so far** mean?
       1. In the future
       2. Up to now
       3. Never
    b. Why do the authors write **so far** twice in the same paragraph?
       1. For repetition
       2. For contrast
       3. For emphasis

19. Read the last paragraph. Who thinks this way about Antarctica?
    a. Only Albert Gore
    b. The authors
    c. Everyone who loves Antarctica

C. Word Forms

Part 1

In English, many verbs become nouns by adding the suffix *-ment*, for example, *improve (v.), improvement (n.).*

Complete each sentence with the correct form of the words on the left. **Use the correct tense of the verbs, in either the affirmative or the negative form. Use the singular or plural form of the nouns.**

employ *(v.)*
employment *(n.)*

1. a. In the past, many companies had very unfair _____ practices.
    b. For example, they _____ anyone they were prejudiced against, and they often made people work six or even seven days a week.

establish *(v.)*
establishment *(n.)*

2. a. The government recently _____ an agency to investigate reports of environmental pollution.
    b. Many private environmental groups praised the government for its timely _____ of this agency.

govern *(v.)*
government *(n.)*

3. a. I'm going to vote for Joan Harrington for mayor because I think that our city _____ needs a change.
    b. I really believe that Joan _____ the city much better than the present mayor has been doing.

manage *(v.)*
management *(n.)*

4. a. Bill and Carla _____ the new Computer Industries company together, beginning next year.
    b. The board of directors believes that the new _____ will help the company improve its productivity over the next five years.

equip *(v.)*
equipment *(n.)*

5. a. The manager of Fielder's Choice always _____ the high school baseball team.
    b. He provides the team with all the basic _____ it needs in return for having his shop's name on the team's uniforms.

In English, many verbs become nouns by adding the suffix *-ion* or *-tion,* for example, *suggest (v.), suggestion (n.).*

Complete each sentence with the correct form of the words on the left. **Use the correct tense of the verbs, in either the affirmative or the negative form. Use the singular or plural form of the nouns.**

reflect *(v.)*
reflection *(n.)*

1. a. The baby saw her _____ in the mirror and smiled.
    b. She didn't understand that the mirror actually _____ her own image, not another child's.

reduce *(v.)*
reduction *(n.)*

2. a. Neil _____ the amount of food he eats because he has gone on a diet.
    b. He is working on a weight _____ of ten to fifteen pounds in a month.

deplete *(v.)*
depletion *(n.)*

3. a. We _____ the world's supply of oil and natural gas at a steady rate.
    b. In order to reduce the rate of _____ of these natural resources, we need to resort to alternate sources of energy.

exploit *(v.)*
exploitation *(n.)*

4. a. If we _____ our natural resources wisely, and take care to protect the environment, we will have a supply of oil and gas for a long time.
    b. However, it is very easy for unwise _____ to leave the Earth both polluted and without resources.

negotiate *(v.)*
negotiation *(n.)*

5. a. The two computer firms entered into serious _____ in order to merge their companies into one.
    b. They not only _____ acceptable terms, but also decided where to relocate the newly formed company.

D. DICTIONARY SKILLS

Choose the appropriate definition for each word. Then write the number and the synonym or meaning in the space provided. Remember that you may need to change the wording of the definition in order to have a grammatically correct sentence.

1.
> **remote** *adj* **1** separated by an interval or space greater than usual **2** far removed in space, time, or relation: divergent **3** out-of-the-way, secluded **4** acting, acted on, or controlled indirectly or from a distance **5** small in degree: slight

Think of a place as (___)_____ as the far side of the moon.

2.
> **contend** *v* **1** to strive or vie in contest or rivalry or against difficulties: struggle **2** to strive in debate: argue **3** maintain, assert **4** to struggle for: contest

Some people (___)_____ that preserving Antarctica as a kind of world park will deprive the rest of the world of oil and mineral reserves.

3.
> **dismiss** *v* **1** to permit or cause to leave **2** to remove from position or service: discharge **3 a** to bar from attention or serious consideration **b** to put out of judicial consideration

Until scientists began the first serious study of Antarctica in 1957, most people (___)_____ the continent. They considered it a vast, useless place.

4.
> **annex** *v* **1** to attach as a quality, consequence, or condition **2** to add to something earlier, larger, or more important **3** to incorporate (a country or other territory) within the domain of a state **4** to obtain or take for oneself

So far, none of the countries claiming sovereignty over Antarctica has moved to formally (___)_____ it.

Read the article a second time. Underline what you think are the main ideas. Then scan the article and complete the following outline, using the sentences that you have underlined to help you. You will use this outline later to answer specific questions about the article.

I.   People with Conflicting Interests in Antarctica

    A.

        reason:

    B.   tourists

        reason: They prize the chance to visit Earth's last frontier

    C.

        reason:

    D.

        reason:

II. The Madrid Protocol

    A.   date:

    B.   original number of participating nations:

    C.   purpose:

III.

    A.

    B.

    C.   Winds blow at more than 200 mph

    D.

    E.   There are no villages, towns, or plants

IV. Antarctica Is Vital to Life on Earth

    A.

    B.

    C.

    D.

V.   The Antarctic Treaty's Purpose

    A.

    B.

    C.

Information Organization Quiz and Summary

Read each question carefully. Use your notes to answer the questions. Do not refer back to the text. Write your answers in the space provided under each question. When you are finished, write a brief summary of the article.

1. Why are there conflicting interests regarding Antarctica?

   _____

   _____

2. What is the Madrid Protocol?

   _____

   _____

3. Describe the continent of Antarctica.

   _____

   _____

4. Is Antarctica necessary to life on Earth? Why, or why not?

   _____

   _____

5. What is the purpose of the Antarctic Treaty?

   _____

   _____

Summary

   _____

   _____

   _____

   _____

G. *Critical Thinking Strategies*

Read each question carefully. Write your response in the space provided. Remember that there is no one correct answer. Your response depends on what **you** think.

1. Read lines 21–23. What do you think would happen if sea levels rose 200 feet?

   _____

   _____

   _____

   _____

2. Read lines 38–41. What do you think are some other reasons that it may be important to study ancient climates?

   _____

   _____

   _____

   _____

3. Read lines 59–64. When the Antarctic Treaty was signed in 1961, very little was known about the continent's natural resources. According to John Splettstoesser, what is the relationship between the quick signing of the treaty and the lack of information about the resources?

   _____

   _____

   _____

   _____

H. *Follow-up Discussion* AND *Writing Activities*

1. Scientists, tourists, environmentalists, and oil and mineral seekers all have different opinions about what to do with Antarctica. Choose one of these four groups, and imagine that you are a member. Working with a partner or in a small group, make a list of reasons why Antarctica is important to your particular group. Compare your list with your classmates' lists. Then as a class decide which group has the strongest reasons to support its point of view.

2. Form a panel of experts. Write a set of guidelines for the protection and use of Antarctica by all the interested countries of the world. You want to be fair to all the interested countries. You also want to try to satisfy the four groups previously mentioned: scientists, environmentalists, tourists, and oil and mineral seekers.

3. The authors ask who Antarctica belongs to. Whose continent *is* Antarctica? Do you think it should belong to one country, many countries, or to no one? Write a composition explaining your opinion.

4. In the third paragraph, the authors say that tourists consider Antarctica to be Earth's last frontier. However, other people do not agree with this statement. They believe that there are other places on Earth that have not yet been fully explored and that are still exciting, challenging places to go to. Alone, or with a partner, decide what other such places exist on Earth and examine why people would be very interested in going there.

5. Reread the fifth paragraph. In this paragraph, the authors describe Antarctica by comparing it with other places and by giving facts about it. The authors are trying to convey an image and a feeling about this unusual continent. Imagine that you keep a journal and that you are visiting Antarctica. **Write a journal entry** in which you describe what you see and how being in Antarctica makes you feel. Do you have feelings similar to those of the first explorers?

Surfing THE *INTERNET*

Antarctica has always fascinated people. Many people have tried to explore it and to reach the South Pole, for example, Robert Falcon Scott and Roald Amundsen, and, most recently, Will Steger and five others. Some of the Antarctica explorers died in their attempts.

Go to the Internet and find information on Antarctica. Read about the explorers who went there. Read the entries they wrote in their diaries. Print out maps and photographs, and prepare a presentation for your class on one of these explorers or groups of explorers.

I. Cloze Quiz

Chapter 10: Antarctica: Whose Continent Is It Anyway?

Read the passage on this page. Fill in the blanks below with one word from the list. Use each word once.

agreement	claims	established	number	science
all	continent	explorations	question	scientists
Antarctica	countries	however	remains	temporarily
Argentina	effect	long	research	useless

Until _____ (1) began the first serious study of the

_____ (2) during the 1957–58 International Geophysical Year (IGY), a

multicountry cooperative _____ (3) project, Antarctica was

dismissed as a vast, _____ (4) continent.

Based upon early _____ (5) and questionable land grants,

seven _____ (6), including Great Britain, Chile, and

_____ (7), claim sovereignty over vast tracts of the continent.

_____ (8), as IGY wound down, the _____ (9) of who owns

_____ (10) came to head. The 12 participating countries reached an

international _____ (11), the Antarctic treaty, which took

_____ (12) in June 1961. The _____ (13) has since grown,

making 39 in _____ (14). It _____ (15) Antarctica as a

"continent for _____ (16) and peace," and _____ (17) sets

aside all _____ (18) of sovereignty for as _____ (19) as the

treaty _____ (20) in effect.

A Messenger From the Past
by James Shreeve

Discover

Prereading Preparation

1. Do you think it's important to learn about humans of the past? Why, or why not?

2. What are some ways we can learn about humans of the past?

3. Read the title of this article and look at the picture. Who is the messenger from the past? What message, or information, can he give us today?

1 His people said good-bye and watched him walk off toward the mountains.
2 They had little reason to fear for his safety: the man was well dressed in
3 insulated clothing and equipped with tools needed to survive the Alpine climate.
4 However, as weeks passed without his return, they must have grown worried,
5 then anxious, and finally resigned. After many years everyone who knew him
6 had died, and not even a memory of the man remained.

7 Then, on an improbably distant day, he came down from the mountain.
8 Things had changed a bit: it wasn't the Bronze Age anymore, and he was a
9 celebrity.

10 When a melting glacier released its hold on a 4,000-year-old corpse in
11 September, it was quite rightly called one of the most important archeological
12 finds of the century. Discovered by a German couple hiking at 10,500 feet in the
13 Italian Tyrol near the Austrian border, the partially freeze-dried body still wore
14 remnants of leather garments and boots that had been stuffed with straw for
15 insulation. The hikers alerted scientists from the University of Innsbruck in
16 Austria, whose more complete examination revealed that the man was tattooed
17 on his back and behind his knee. At his side was a bronze ax of a type typical in
18 southern central Europe around 2000 B.C. On his expedition—perhaps to hunt
19 or to search for metal ore—he had also carried an all-purpose stone knife, a
20 wooden backpack, a bow and a quiver, a small bag containing a flint lighter and
21 kindling, and an arrow repair kit in a leather pouch.

22 Such everyday gear gives an unprecedented perspective on life in early
23 Bronze Age Europe. "The most exciting thing is that we genuinely appear to be
24 looking at a man who had some kind of accident in the course of a perfectly
25 ordinary trip," says archeologist Ian Kinnes of the British Museum. "These are
26 not artifacts placed in a grave, but the fellow's own possessions."

27 Unlike the Egyptians and Mesopotamians of the time, who had more
28 advanced civilizations with cities and central authority, the Ice Man and his
29 countrymen lived in a society built around small, stable villages. He probably
30 spoke in a tongue ancestral to current European languages. Furthermore,
31 though he was a member of a farming culture, he may well have been hunting,
32 when he died, to add meat to his family's diet. X-rays of the quiver showed that
33 it contained 14 arrows. While his backpack was empty, careful exploration of
34 the trench where he died revealed remnants of animal skin and bones at the
35 same spot where the pack lay. There was also the remainder of a pile of berries.
36 Clearly the man didn't starve to death.

37 So why did the Ice Man die? The trench provided him with shelter from
38 the elements, and he also had a braided mat of grass to keep him warm. If injury
39 or illness caused the Ice Man's death, an autopsy on the 4,000-year-old victim

could turn up some clues. The circumstances of his death may have preserved such evidence, as well as other details of his life. Freeze-dried by the frigid climate, his inner organs and other soft tissues are much better preserved than those of dried-up Egyptian mummies or the waterlogged Scandinavian "Bog Men" found in recent years.

One concern, voiced by archeologist Colin Renfrew of Cambridge University, is that the hot TV lights that greeted the hunter's return to civilization may have damaged these fragile tissues, jeopardizing a chance to recover additional precious genetic information from his chromosomes. If not, Renfrew says, "it may be possible to get very long DNA sequences out of this material. This is far and away the most exciting aspect of the discovery."

For the time being, all biological research has literally been put on ice at the University of Innsbruck while an international team of experts, led by researcher Konrad Spindler, puzzles out a way to thaw the body without destroying it. As sensational as it sounds, it remains to be seen how useful 4,000-year-old human DNA will really be. "The problem is that we are dealing with a single individual," says evolutionary biologist Robert Sokal of the State University of New York at Stony Brook. "In order to make statements about the population that existed at the time, we need more specimens."

The wish for more messengers from the past may yet come true. Five more bodies of mountain climbers, all of whom died within the past 50 years, have emerged from melting Austrian mountain ice this summer. The Ice Man's return from the Tyrol has demonstrated that the local climate is warmer now than it has been for 4,000 years. People are beginning to wonder—and plan for—what the melting ice may reveal next.

"No one ever thought this could happen," says Christopher Stringer, an anthropologist at the Natural History Museum in London. "The fact that it has occurred once means that people will now be looking for it again."

Equipment Found with the Ice Man of Tyrol

Dagger with Woven Bag   Bronze-Blade Ax   Bear Hat   Bow and Arrows with Quiver   Woven Clothing   Leggings

Fact-Finding Exercise

Read the passage once. Then read the following statements. Scan the article quickly to find out if each statement is true (T) or false (F). If a statement is false, change it so that it is true.

1. ____ T ____ F   The Ice Man lived 4,000 years ago.

_____

2. ____ T ____ F   The Ice Man was discovered in Europe by scientists.

_____

3. ____ T ____ F   Scientists aren't sure how the Ice Man died.

_____

4. ____ T ____ F   The Ice Man's body had been frozen for 4,000 years.

_____

5. ____ T ____ F   Scientists have examined the Ice Man to get genetic information.

_____

6. ____ T ____ F   More bodies of mountain climbers who died 4,000 years ago were discovered.

_____

Reading Analysis

Read each question carefully. Circle the number or letter of the correct answer, or write your answer in the space provided.

1. Read lines 7 and 9. This statement means
   a. the Ice Man walked down from the mountain
   b. the Ice Man woke up on the mountain
   c. the Ice Man's body was brought down from the mountain

2. In line 10, what does the **4,000-year-old corpse** refer to?

   _____

3. Read lines 15–17. **Whose** refers to
   a. the Ice Man
   b. the scientists
   c. the hikers

4. Read lines 17–22.
   a. What are some examples of the Ice Man's **everyday gear?**

   _____

   _____

   b. **Gear** means
      1. clothes
      2. equipment
      3. weapons

5. Read lines 29–30. In this sentence, what does **tongue** refer to?
   a. The Ice Man's mouth
   b. The Ice Man's accent
   c. The Ice Man's language

6. In line 30, what follows **furthermore?**

   a. An example

   b. A theory

   c. Additional information

7. Read line 36. What does **clearly** mean?

   a. Unfortunately

   b. Obviously

   c. Possibly

8. Read lines 40–41.

   a. What does **evidence** mean?

      1. Proof of how the Ice Man died

      2. Clues to how the Ice Man died

      3. Theories describing how the Ice Man may have died

   b. What does **as well as** mean?

      1. Better than

      2. As good as

      3. In addition to

9. Read lines 40–44. What are the Ice Man's **inner organs and other soft tissues?**

   a. Parts of his body

   b. Objects he had with him

   c. The food remaining in his stomach

10. In line 50, **far and away** indicates

   a. distance

   b. importance

   c. excitement

11. Read lines 51–54.

   a. **For the time being** means

      1. for a long time.

      2. for now.

      3. for a human being.

   b. **Thaw** means

      1. melt, as ice becomes water.

      2. bring back to life.

      3. bring back to normal temperature.

12. In line 59, **yet** means
    a. still
    b. but
    c. not

13. Read lines 66–67. What does **it** refer to?

    _____

    _____

C. Word Forms

Part 1

In English, many verbs become nouns by adding the suffix *-ion* or *-tion*, for example, *stimulate (v.)*, *stimulation (n.)*.

Complete each sentence with the correct form of the words on the left. **Use the correct tense of the verbs, in either the affirmative or the negative form. Use the singular or plural form of the nouns.**

insulate *(v.)*
insulation *(n.)*

1. a. Nicholas put fiberglass between the outside and inside walls of his house in order to provide good _____.
   b. He also _____ the roof with fiberglass; consequently, he saved money on his heating bills last winter.

demonstrate *(v.)*
demonstration *(n.)*

2. a. Many power companies provide clear and simple _____ to their customers on how to save on utility and heating bills.
   b. The companies _____ how to insulate a home and what types of light bulbs and air conditioners save electricity.

explore *(v.)*
exploration *(n.)*

3. a. When we go on vacation, we _____ the Adirondack Mountains on foot.
   b. As part of our extensive _____ , we are going to investigate some underground caverns too.

preserve *(v.)*
preservation *(n.)*

4. a. Many people are interested in the permanent _____ of undeveloped land in Alaska.
   b. If we _____ this land now, it will be exploited by major oil companies.

destroy *(v.)*

destruction *(n.)*

5. a. Eddie was accused of willful _____ of property when he threw a rock through his neighbor's window.

b. He apparently _____ the window after he had an argument with his neighbor.

Part 2

In English, the noun and verb forms of some words are the same, for example, *promise (v.), promise (n.)*.

Complete each sentence with the correct form of the words on the left. **Use the correct tense of the verbs, in either the affirmative or the negative form. Use the singular or plural form of the nouns. In addition, indicate whether you are using the verb *(v.)* or the noun *(n.)* form of the word.**

alert

1. a. The police department put the town on _____ after *(v., n.)* a criminal escaped from the nearby prison.

b. After they _____ everyone, they began a systematic *(v., n.)* search of the area in order to find the escaped convict.

repair

2. a. I called in a plumber to fix the leak under my kitchen sink, but he _____ the leak properly, and water *(v., n.)* continued to drip.

b. I decided to buy a book on plumbing and I made the _____ myself. *(v., n.)*

return

3. a. Perry is going to the store now, but he _____ by *(v., n.)* 6 o'clock. He is going to take back a shirt that doesn't fit.

b. The store accepts both _____ and exchanges. Perry *(v., n.)* wants an exchange; he wants the same shirt, but in the correct size.

release

4. a. Film companies in the United States usually _____
about 20 major films a year. _(v., n.)_

b. They always advertise their new _____ on
_(v., n.)_
television and radio, and in magazines.

damage

5. a. The flood caused considerable property _____ to
homes near the river. _(v., n.)_

b. The muddy water ruined many people's homes, but,
fortunately, it _____ any major buildings or
_(v., n.)_
contaminate the water supply.

D. DICTIONARY SKILLS

Choose the appropriate definition for each word. Then write the number and the synonym or meaning in the space provided. Remember that you may need to change the wording of the definition in order to have a grammatically correct sentence.

1.

> **remnant** *n* **1 a** a usually small part, member, or trace remaining **b** a small surviving group **2** an unsold or unused end of piece goods

The Ice Man's body still wore (___)_____ of leather garments and boots that been stuffed with straw for insulation.

2.

> **ordinary** *adj* **1** of a kind to be expected in the normal order of events: routine, usual **2** having or constituting immediate or original jurisdiction **3 a** of common quality, rank or ability **b** deficient in quality: poor, inferior

The Ice Man had some kind of accident in the course of a perfectly (___)_____ trip.

3.

> **stable** *adj* **1 a** firmly established: fixed, steadfast **b** not changing or fluctuating: unvarying **c** permanent, enduring **2 a** steady in purpose: firm in resolution **b** not subject to insecurity or emotional illness: sane, rational **3** not readily altering in chemical makeup or physical state

The Ice Man and his countrymen lived in a society built around small, (___)_____ villages.

4.

> **element** *n* **1 a** any of the four substances
> air, water, fire, and earth formerly believed to
> compose the physical universe **b** *pl:*
> weather conditions caused by activities of the
> elements; *esp:* violent or severe weather
> **2 a** a basic member of a mathematical or
> logical class or set **b** one of the necessary
> data or values on which calculations or
> conclusions are based

The trench provided the Ice Man with shelter from the
(___)_____, and he also had a braided mat of grass to
keep him warm.

Read the article a second time. Underline what you think are the main ideas. Then scan the article and complete the following flowchart, using the sentences that you have underlined to help you. For each possible cause of death, indicate *yes, no,* or *maybe,* based on your reasoning from the information in the text. You will use this flowchart later to answer specific questions about the article.

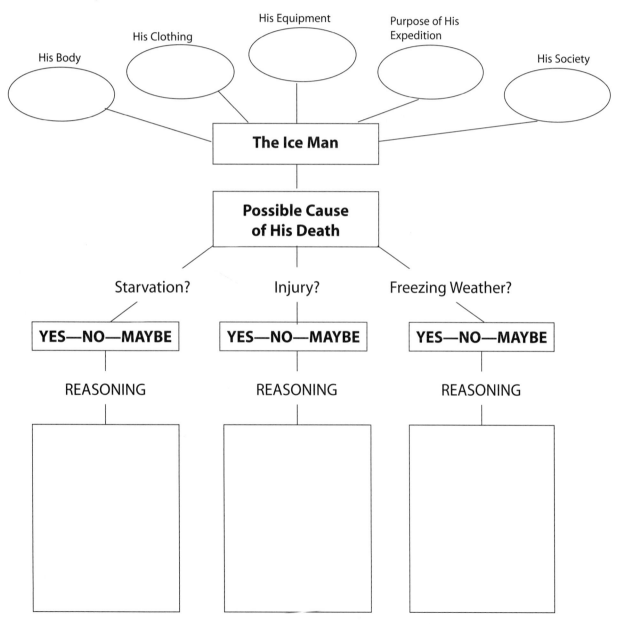

Read each question carefully. Use your notes to answer the questions. Do not refer back to the text. Write your answers in the space provided under each question. When you are finished, write a brief summary of the article.

1. a. What was the Ice Man wearing when he was found?

    _____

    b. What marks did the Ice Man have on his body?

    _____

    _____

2. a. What did the Ice Man have with him?

    _____

    _____

    b. What might he have been doing before he died?

    _____

    _____

3. Describe the society that the Ice Man lived in.

    _____

    _____

4. What are some clues as to how the Ice Man died?

    _____

    _____

Summary

_____

_____

_____

_____

_____

G. Critical Thinking Strategies

Read each question carefully. Write your response in the space provided. Remember that there is no one correct answer. Your response depends on what **you** think.

1. In the first paragraph of the article, the author gives a personalized description of what happened to the Ice Man 4,000 years ago and how his friends and family may have felt about his loss. What do you think the tone or feeling of this paragraph is? How is the tone and style different from the rest of the article? Why do you think the author started the article in this way?

_____

_____

_____

_____

2. In the third paragraph, James Shreeve writes that the discovery of the Ice Man "was quite rightly called one of the most important archeological finds of the century." What do you think Shreeve's opinion of this discovery is? Why do you think so?

_____

_____

_____

_____

3. In describing the equipment that the Ice Man had with him, Ian Kinnes points out that they "are not artifacts placed in a grave, but the fellow's own possessions." Why do you think this is so important? Why might objects in a grave be different from what a man normally carries with him for a day or a week?

_____

_____

_____

_____

4. In lines 27–32, the author describes the society that the Ice Man lived in and compares it with the civilizations of the Egyptians and Mesopotamians of the same time period. How do you think James Shreeve knows what the Ice Man's society was like? How does he know what Egyptian and Mesopotamian society was like at that time?

_____

_____

_____

_____

5. The article informs us that "the Ice Man's return from the Tyrol has demonstrated that the local climate is warmer now than it has been for 4,000 years." What inferences can we make from this statement? What do you think may happen in the future as a result of a warmer climate?

_____

_____

_____

_____

H. *Follow-up Discussion* AND *Writing Activities*

1. According to Robert Sokal, an evolutionary biologist at the State University of New York at Stony Brook, we need to find many examples of preserved people from 4,000 years ago in order to "make statements about the population that existed at the time." What information do you think we can learn from such discoveries? How might this information be useful to us in the twentieth century?

2. If you could ask the Ice Man questions about himself and his time, what would you ask? Work with a partner and make a list of questions. Compare your list with your classmates' lists.

3. Image that you were the Ice Man 4,000 years ago. **Write a journal or diary entry** of your last week alive. Describe what you did, where you went, the people you met, and your last hours alive.

Surfing THE *INTERNET*

The article titled "Messenger from the Past" was written before scientists published the results of their study on the Ice Man and his possessions. More recent articles will have more detailed information. They may also contain some revised information on the Ice Man, because some of the guesses that scientists made initially may have been incorrect.

1. a. Look on the Internet for a recent article on the Ice Man. Print out the article. Read it and bring it to class.

   b. In small groups, refer to the following table. With the up-to-date information your group now has, check the information from the article "Messenger from the Past." If the information is correct, leave it. If the information has been shown to be incorrect, change it.

	Original Information (Source): "Messenger from the Past"— *Discover*	**Revised Information (Source):**
When the Ice Man lived	4,000 years ago	
The Age the Ice Man lived in	the Bronze Age	
The Ice Man's age at death	(unknown)	
The Ice Man's physical condition	uninjured	
The marks on the Ice Man's body	tattoos on his back and behind his knee	
The Ice Man's equipment	1. clothes made of leather 2. a bronze ax 3. a bow, arrows, and a quiver	

c. Compare your table with your classmates' tables. Which article(s) had the most detailed and correct information?

2. According to this article, the Ice Man lived 4,000 years ago in the Bronze Age. His society was very different from the civilizations of Egypt and Mesopotamia of the same time period. Select an area of the world, perhaps your own. Refer to the Internet, a history book or an encyclopedia, or your own knowledge. Write a description of what life was like 5,000 years ago for the people in the society you have chosen. Discuss how their lives and the lives of Ice Man and his people were similar and how they were different.

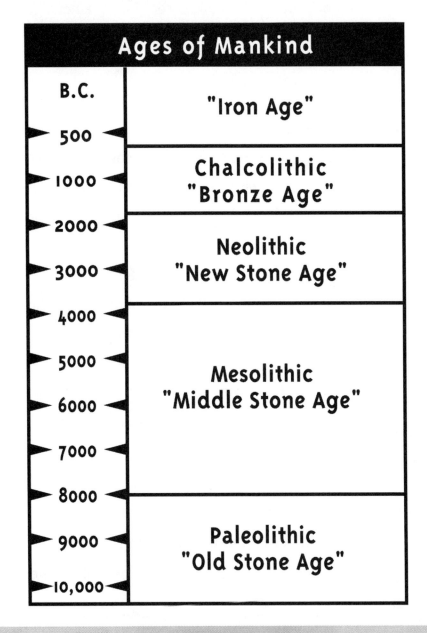

Chapter 11: A Messenger from the Past

Read the passage on this page. Fill in the blanks below with one word from the list above the passage. Use each word once.

ancestral	clearly	die	hunting	revealed
authority	contained	evidence	illness	society
circumstances	culture	exploration	probably	starve
civilizations	details	furthermore	remainder	unlike

_____ the Egyptians and Mesopotamians of the time,
(1)
who had more advanced _____ with cities and central
(2)
_____, the Ice Man and his countrymen lived in a
(3)
_____ built around small, stable villages. He _____
(4)   (5)
spoke in a tongue _____ to current European languages.
(6)
_____, though he was a member of a farming
(7)
_____, he may well have been _____, when he died,
(8)   (9)
to add meat to his family's diet. X-rays of the quiver showed that it

_____ 14 arrows. While his backpack was empty, careful
(10)
_____ of the trench where he died _____ remnants
(11)   (12)
of animal skin and bones at the same spot where the pack lay. There was also

the _____ of a pile of berries. _____ the man didn't
(13)   (14)
_____ to death.
(15)

So why did the Ice Man _____? If injury or
(16)
_____ caused the Ice Man's death, an autopsy on the 4,000-year-
(17)
old victim could turn up some clues. The _____ of his death may
(18)
have preserved such _____, as well as other _____
(19)   (20)
of his life.

Is Time Travel Possible?

by Mark Davidson

USA Today

Prereading Preparation

1. What is **time travel?**

2. Do you think time travel may be possible? Why, or why not?

3. Do you think scientists should try to find a way to travel to the past? To the future? Why, or why not?

4. Would you like to travel to the past? If you would, where would you go?

5. Would you like to travel to the future? If you would, where would you go? Using the chart below, take a survey of your classmates. Compare your classmates' responses.

Student's Name	Would you like to travel to the past? Yes/No	Where would you like to go in the past?	Would you like to travel to the future? Yes/No	Where would you like to go in the future?

Is Time Travel Possible?

1   Contrary to the old warning that time waits for no one, time slows down
2 when you are on the move. It also slows down more as you move faster, which
3 means astronauts someday may survive so long in space that they would return
4 to an Earth of the distant future. If you could move at the speed of light, 186,282
5 miles a second, your time would stand still. If you could move faster than light,
6 your time would move backward.
7   Although no form of matter yet discovered moves as fast or faster than
8 light, scientific experiments have confirmed that accelerated motion causes a
9 voyager's, or traveler's, time to be stretched. Albert Einstein predicted this in

1905, when he introduced the concept of relative time as part of his Special Theory of Relativity. A search is now under way to confirm the suspected existence of particles of matter that move faster than light and therefore possibly might serve as our passports to the past.

An obsession with time—saving, gaining, wasting, losing, and mastering it—seems to have been part of humanity for as long as humans have existed. Humanity also has been obsessed with trying to capture the *meaning* of time. Einstein used a definition of time, for experimental purposes, as that which is measured by a clock. Thus, time and time's relativity are measurable by any sundial, hourglass, metronome, alarm clock, or an atomic clock that can measure a billionth of a second.

Scientists have demonstrated that an ordinary airplane flight is like a brief visit to the Fountain of Youth. In 1972, for example, scientists who took four atomic clocks on an airplane trip around the world discovered that the moving clocks moved slightly slower than atomic clocks which had remained on the ground. If you fly around the world, preferably going eastward to gain the advantage of the added motion of the Earth's rotation, the atomic clocks show that you'll return younger than you would have been if you had stayed home. Frankly, you'll be younger by only 40 billionths of a second. Even such an infinitesimal saving of time proves that time can be stretched. Moreover, atomic clocks have demonstrated that the stretching of time increases with speed.

Here is an example of what you can expect if tomorrow's space-flight technology enables you to move at ultrahigh speeds. Imagine you're an astronaut with a twin who stays home.[1] If you travel back and forth to the nearest star at about half the speed of light, you'll be gone for 18 Earth years. When you return, your twin will be 18 years older, but you'll have aged only 16 years. Your body will be two years younger than your twin's because time aboard the flying spaceship will have moved more slowly than time on Earth. You will have aged normally, but you have been in a slower time zone. If your spaceship moves at about 90% of lightspeed, you'll age only 50% as much as your twin. If you whiz along at 99.86% of lightspeed, you'll age only five percent as much. These examples of time-stretching, of course, cannot be tested with any existing spacecraft. They are based on mathematical projections of relativity science.

Speed is not the only factor that slows time; so does gravity. Einstein determined in his General Theory of Relativity that the force of an object's gravity "curves" the space in the object's gravitational field. When gravity curves space, Einstein reasoned, gravity also must curve time, because space and time are linked.

[1]This hypothetical situation is known as the Twin Paradox.

Numerous atomic clock experiments have confirmed Einstein's calculation that the closer you are to the Earth's center of gravity, which is the Earth's core, the slower you will age. In one of these experiments, an atomic clock was taken from the National Bureau of Standards in Washington, D.C., near sea level, and moved to mile-high Denver. The results demonstrated that people in Denver age more rapidly by a tiny amount than people in Washington.

If you would like gravity's space-time warp to extend your life, get a home at the beach and a job as a deep-sea diver. Avoid living in the mountains or working in a skyscraper. That advice, like the advice about flying around the world, will enable you to slow your aging by only a few billionths of a second. Nevertheless, those tiny fractions of a second add up to more proof that time-stretching is a reality.

Time Reversal

According to scientific skeptics, time reversal—travel to the past—for humans would mean an unthinkable reversal of cause and effect. This reversal would permit you to do something in the past that changes the present. The skeptics worry that you even might commit an act that prevents your own birth.

Some scientists believe we should keep an open mind about time reversal. Open-minders speculate that time-travelers who change the past would be opening doors to *alternative* histories, rather than interfering with history as we know it. For example, if you prevented the assassination of Abraham Lincoln, then a new line of historical development would be created. The alternative history—the one without Lincoln's assassination—would have a completely separate, ongoing existence. Thus, no change would be made in anybody's existing history. Another possibility is that nature might have an unbreakable law preventing time travelers from changing the past.

Journey to the Future

If we did discover a source of energy that would enable us to travel beyond lightspeed, we might have access not only to the past, but also to the future. Suppose you went on a super-lightspeed trek to the Spiral Nebula in the Andromeda Galaxy. That location is separated from Earth by 1,500,000 lightyears, the distance light travels in 1,500,000 years. Suppose you make the round trip in just a few moments. If all goes well, you'll return to the Earth 3,000,000 years into its future, because that's how much Earth time will have elapsed.

Time is an abstraction. In other words, it cannot be seen, touched, smelled, or tasted. It seems to have no existence apart from the events it measures, but something tells us that time is out there, somewhere. "When we pursue the

85 meaning of time," according to the time-obsessed English novelist-playwright
86 J. B. Priestly, "we are like a knight on a quest, condemned to wander through
87 innumerable forests, bewildered and baffled, because the magic beast he is
88 looking for is the horse he is riding."

89   What about our quest for particles that travel faster than light? If we find
90 them, will we be able to control their energy to tour the past? If we return to
91 our past, will we be forced to repeat our mistakes and suffer the same
92 consequences? Or will we be able to use our experience to make everything turn
93 out better the second time around?

94   Will we ever be able to take instant trips to the distant future, the way
95 people do in the movies, with a twist of a dial and a "Zap!, Zap!" of sound effects?
96 One cannot resist the temptation to respond that only time will tell.

Fact-Finding Exercise

Read the passage once. Then read the following statements. Scan the article quickly to find out if each statement is true (T) or false (F). If a statement is false, change it so that it is true.

1. ＿＿ T ＿＿ F   If you could move at the speed of light, your time would move backward.

＿＿＿＿＿＿＿＿＿＿＿＿＿＿＿＿＿＿＿＿＿＿＿＿＿＿＿＿

2. ＿＿ T ＿＿ F   Scientists have discovered a form of matter that moves as fast as light.

＿＿＿＿＿＿＿＿＿＿＿＿＿＿＿＿＿＿＿＿＿＿＿＿＿＿＿＿

3. ＿＿ T ＿＿ F   Scientists have done experiments which show that the stretching of time increases with speed.

＿＿＿＿＿＿＿＿＿＿＿＿＿＿＿＿＿＿＿＿＿＿＿＿＿＿＿＿

4. ＿＿ T ＿＿ F   Both speed and gravity slow time.

＿＿＿＿＿＿＿＿＿＿＿＿＿＿＿＿＿＿＿＿＿＿＿＿＿＿＿＿

5. ＿＿ T ＿＿ F   The closer you are to the Earth's core, the faster you will age.

＿＿＿＿＿＿＿＿＿＿＿＿＿＿＿＿＿＿＿＿＿＿＿＿＿＿＿＿

6. ＿＿ T ＿＿ F   Some people worry that if you could go back in time, you might change the present.

＿＿＿＿＿＿＿＿＿＿＿＿＿＿＿＿＿＿＿＿＿＿＿＿＿＿＿＿

Reading Analysis

Read each question carefully. Circle the number or letter of the correct answer, or write your answer in the space provided.

1. Read lines 4–6.

   a. What is the speed of light?

   _____

   b. What does **your time would stand still** mean?
      1. Your time would speed up.
      2. Your time would reverse.
      3. Your time would stop.

2. Read lines 9–10: "Einstein predicted **this** in 1905." What does **this** refer to? In other words, what did Einstein predict?

   _____

   _____

3. Read lines 11–13.

   a. **Under way** means that the search is
      1. being done now
      2. finished
      3. under a method

   b. **Suspected existence** means that
      1. people have found these particles
      2. people believe these particles exist
      3. people do not believe these particles exist

   c. What are our **passports to the past?**

   _____

4. Read lines 21–22. In this sentence, scientists mean that an airplane trip might
   a. make you younger
   b. slow down the aging process
   c. make you older

5. Read line 28. **Frankly** means
   a. actually
   b. on the contrary
   c. obviously

6. In lines 28–29, an **infinitesimal** saving of time is
   a. a large amount
   b. an average amount
   c. a very small amount

7. In lines 31–32, **tomorrow** refers to
   a. the day after today
   b. some time in the future
   c. some time next year

8. Read lines 31–36.
   a. What is this imaginary situation commonly known as?

   _____

   b. How do you know?

   _____

   c. **Back and forth** means
      1. travel to the nearest star and then return to Earth
      2. travel to the nearest star two times
      3. travel back to the nearest star after you've been there

9. Read lines 40–41. **Whiz** means
   a. age
   b. change
   c. move

10. Read lines 44–46. Why is **"curves"** in quotation marks?

   _____

11. Read lines 68–72. What is this imaginary situation an example of?

   _____

12. Read lines 74–75. What is the purpose of **did?**
    a. To ask a question
    b. To show emphasis
    c. To express the past

13. In line 79, what does **round trip** mean?

    _____

14. Read lines 84–88.
    a. What does **quest** mean?

    _____

    b. How do you know?

    _____

C. Word Forms

Part 1

In English, some verbs become adjectives by adding the suffix -al, for example, *cause (v.), causal (adj.)*.

Complete each sentence with the correct form of the words on the left. **Use the correct tense of the verbs, in either the affirmative or the negative form.**

experiment *(v.)*
experimental *(adj.)*

1. a. Scientists in the pharmaceutical laboratory are working on a new drug, but it is in the _____ stage. Doctors cannot prescribe it yet.

    b. The scientists _____ successfully with the drug in the laboratory; now they need to test it on human volunteers.

cause *(v.)*
causal *(adj.)*

2. a. When researchers try to establish what _____ a given disease, they look for relationships between certain factors and the onset of the disease.

    b. Sometimes it is quite difficult to establish a clear _____ relationship between the disease and a particular factor.

survive *(v.)*
survival *(adj.)*

3. a. Mark and Laura were stranded in the mountains in the middle of a severe snowstorm. They needed basic _____ skills in order to stay alive.

    b. They only _____ the bitter cold because they found a small cave, which protected them from the harsh weather until a rescue team found them two days later.

arrive *(v.)*
arrival *(adj.)*

4. a. All international passengers must go through the _____ gate into customs before leaving the airport.

    b. Everyone who _____ at the airport must declare what they are bringing into the country.

In English, some verbs become nouns by adding the suffix *-ance* or *-ence,* for example, *appear (v.), appearance (n.).*

Complete each sentence with the correct form of the words on the left. **Use the correct tense of the verbs, in either the affirmative or the negative form.**

avoid *(v.)*
avoidance *(n.)*

1. a. Monica regularly _____ exposure to the sun.
    b. Her careful _____ of the sun is due to persistent skin problems.

resist *(v.)*
resistance *(n.)*

2. a. It is a well-known fact that stress lowers the body's _____ to illness.
    b. It is logical, then, that we _____ disease better when we maintain good health and avoid stressful situations.

accept *(v.)*
acceptance *(n.)*

3. a. Gloria's English teacher _____ any papers that are more than two days late. This is her policy.
    b. Her professor's _____ of papers also depends on whether the students have followed her guidelines for the format of the paper, such as double spacing.

insist *(v.)*
insistence *(n.)*

4. a. Arthur invariably _____ on having dinner at the same time every day.
    b. His odd _____ on the same dinnertime isn't his only habit. He also insists on eating the same breakfast, and going to the same place for vacation every year.

exist *(v.)*
existence *(n.)*

5. a. There is a myth about a creature called the Abominable Snowman, which some people believe _____ somewhere in the Himalaya Mountains.
    b. There is also a legend about the _____ of a giant creature called Sasquatch, or Bigfoot, which supposedly lives in the Pacific Northwest.

D. DICTIONARY SKILLS

Choose the appropriate definition for each word. Then write the number and the synonym or meaning in the space provided. Remember that you may need to change the wording of the definition in order to have a grammatically correct sentence.

1.

> **matter** *n* **1 a** a subject under consideration.
> **b** a subject of disagreement **c** the subject or substance of a discourse or writing
> **d** problem; difficulty **2 a** the substance of which a physical object is composed
> **b** material substance that occupies space and has weight **3** something written or printed
> **4** a more or less definite amount or quantity

No form of (___)_____ has yet been discovered that moves as fast or faster than light.

2.

> **stretch** *v* **1** to extend (as one's limbs or body) in a reclining position **2** to reach out: extend **3** to extend in length **4 a** to enlarge or distend esp. by force **b** to extend or expand as if by physical force **c** strain
> **5** to cause to reach or continue (as from one point to another or across a space)

Experiments with atomic clocks show that it is possible to (___)_____ time.

3.

> **determine** *v* **1 a** to fix conclusively or authoritatively **b** to decide by judicial sentence **c** to settle or decide by choice of alternatives or possibilities **d** resolve **2 a** to fix the form, position, or character of beforehand **b** to bring about as a result: regulate **3 a** to find out or come to a decision about by investigation, reasoning, or calculation **b** to discover the taxonomic position or the generic and specific names of

Einstein (___)_____ in his General Theory of Relativity that the force of an object's gravity "curves" the space in the object's gravitational field.

4.

> **speculate** *v* **1 a** to meditate on or ponder a
> subject: reflect **b** to review something idly
> or casually and often inconclusively
> **2** to assume a business risk in hope of gain

Open-minders (___)_____ that time-travelers who
change the past would be opening doors to alternative histories, rather
than interfering with known history.

Information Organization

Read the article a second time. Underline what you think are the main ideas. Then scan the article and complete the following table, using the sentences that you have underlined to help you. You will use this table later to answer specific questions about the article. Not all the boxes will be filled in.

	Speed	Gravity
Time speeds up		
Time slows down		
Time stops		
Experimental evidence		
Hypothetical example		

Information Organization Quiz and Summary

Read each question carefully. Use your notes to answer the questions. Do not refer back to the text. Write your answers in the space provided under each question. When you are finished, write a brief summary of the article.

1. How does the speed of light affect time?

    _____

    _____

2. Describe the evidence which shows that time is affected by speed.

    _____

    _____

3. Describe the evidence which shows that time is affected by gravity.

    _____

    _____

4. How would time reversal change cause and effect?

    _____

    _____

Summary

_____

_____

_____

_____

_____

G. *Critical Thinking* Strategies

Read each question carefully. Write your response in the space provided. Remember that there is no one correct answer. Your response depends on what **you** think.

1. In line 1, the author refers to a proverb, "Time waits for no one." What do you think this proverb means? Why do you think the author mentioned this proverb with regard to the topic of the reading?

    _____

    _____

    _____

2. Read lines 41–43. Why do you think time-stretching cannot be tested with any spacecraft we have today?

    _____

    _____

    _____

3. Read lines 61–64. What do you think **reversal of cause and effect** means? What do you think about this argument against travel to the past?

    _____

    _____

    _____

4. Read lines 82–88. What do you think is the purpose of this reference to a knight on a quest? In other words, what image do you think the author wants us to visualize? Why?

    _____

    _____

    _____

H. *Follow-up Discussion* AND *Writing Activities*

1. Imagine that you could travel to the past. What is the one historical event you would like to change? Why do you want to change it? How would you change it? What consequences might this change have for the present?

2. Would you like to see the future? Why? What year do you want to visit? Explain.

3. Imagine that time travel is possible. Do you think there should be restrictions on this type of travel? For example, many countries have visa and immigration restrictions. Should there also be restrictions on time travel? If so, what restrictions do you suggest? Who would be in charge of making these rules and enforcing them?

4. a. Refer to the Time Preference Survey on page 252. Discuss it in class to make sure you understand the questions.

   b. After you have read the questionnaire, go outside your class alone or in pairs. Survey two or three people.

   c. Bring back your data and combine it with the other students' information. Create a bar graph or other chart to compile your data. Divide your responses by past, present, and future. Then divide those responses by gender and/or by age. What do you observe about the responses? Are there any observable patterns by gender or by age? Speculate on the reasons why these groups prefer a particular time.

5. **Write in your journal.** Imagine that you could travel back in time. Choose a person from the past you'd like to meet. Explain why you would like to meet this person.

Time Preference Survey			
	1	**2**	**3**
Informant's Sex (M/F)			
Informant's Age Group (under 20/20–25/26–30/ 31–35/36–40/41+)			
1. If you could travel through time, when would it be? the past/ stay in the present/ the future			
2. If you prefer the past, why would you go back?			
3. If you prefer the present, why would you stay here?			
4. If you prefer the future, why would you go there?			

Cloze Quiz

Chapter 12: Is Time Travel Possible?

Read the passage on this page. Fill in the blanks below with one word from the list. Use each word once.

concept	future	part	space	than
contrary	light	predicted	speed	time
experiments	motion	return	still	waits
faster	move	slows	survive	yet

_____ to the old warning that time _____ for
(1)   (2)

no one, _____ slows down when you are on the move. It also
(3)

_____ down more as you move _____, which
(4)   (5)

means astronauts someday may _____ so long in
(6)

_____ that they would _____ to an Earth of the
(7)   (8)

distant _____. If you could move at the _____ of
(9)   (10)

light, 186,282 miles a second, your time would stand _____. If
(11)

you could move faster _____ light, your time would
(12)

_____ backward.
(13)

Although no form of matter _____ discovered moves as
(14)

fast or faster than _____ , scientific _____ have
(15)   (16)

confirmed that accelerated _____ causes a voyager's, or
(17)

traveler's, time to be stretched. Albert Einstein _____ this in
(18)

1905, when he introduced the _____ of relative time as
(19)

_____ of his Special Theory of Relativity.
(20)

Unit IV Review

J.   Crossword Puzzle

Read the clues on the next page. Write the answers in the correct spaces in the puzzle.

Crossword Clues

Across

3. The same

4. The past tense of **put**

5. The Ice Man had an _____ made of copper.

6. A dead body

8. The past tense of **write**

10. Our house has _____ in the walls to help keep it warm in the winter.

13. The two countries want to _____ a peace treaty.

18. The past tense of **come**

19. The police look for clues, or _____, to help them solve crimes.

20. The universe is made up of _____.

Down

1. Harry is on a _____ to find the truth.

2. In addition

5. _____ is the coldest place on Earth.

7. Usual; routine

9. Is it possible to _____, or extend, time?

11. People often _____, or wonder, about the possibility of time travel.

12. Many scientists believe in the _____ of life on other planets.

14. We need a lot of gear, or _____, when we go camping in the woods.

15. Many businesses around the world would like to _____ Antarctica's natural resources.

16. The middle of the desert is a very _____ and lonely place.

17. Area; location

1. Modern technology has given us insights into the past, the present, and the future. What do you think is the greatest technological advance we have made so far? How will it help us better understand the past, the present, and the future?

2. If time travel to the past were possible today, it would be very easy for us to learn about ancient civilizations. Image that time travel to the future is also possible. What do you think would be the biggest advantage to knowing the future? What would be the biggest disadvantage? Explain your answer.

3. Imagine that you could travel 500 years into the future in Antarctica. What do you think you would see there? What country or countries would "own" Antarctica? Why? Explain your answer.

4. People sometimes want to save a "picture" of the time they live in for people in the future to see. They select objects to preserve so that people can look at them at a specific time in the future. A time capsule is a sealed container that people use in order to preserve these objects. You are a member of a committee whose job it is to prepare a time capsule for this year. The time capsule will not be opened until the year 3000. Discuss with the other members of your committee what you would like to put into the time capsule in order to show what this year was like.

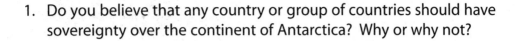
1. Do you believe that any country or group of countries should have sovereignty over the continent of Antarctica? Why or why not?

2. Read the questions and watch the video. Then answer the questions in groups and discuss your answers with the whole class.
   a. What is the climate like on Antarctica? How cold does it get there? How high do the wind speeds get?
   b. So far, no exploration for oil and minerals has occurred in Antarctica. Why not?
   c. Should the ban on exploration continue? Should it be made permanent? What are the pros and cons of this kind of exploration?
   d. If the environment of Antarctica is damaged or polluted, can it recover quickly? For example, how did the oil tanker spill affect the wildlife there?
   e. What is the Wellington Convention? Does it allow exploration for oil and minerals?

3. What predictions can you make about the future of Antarctica? For instance, do you think tourism will expand there? Is it safe to allow tourism to develop? Would you visit Antarctica if you could?

INFOTRAC® Research Activity
COLLEGE EDITION
The Online Library

Recently, research on the Ice Man of Tyrol, nicknamed Oetzi, has determined that he lived 5,300 years ago. Research has also uncovered new information about how Oetzi died. Do a group research project about him. Using InfoTrac, type in "Oetzi" and "mummies; research" and find several articles about how he was discovered and how he died. Each member of the group should read and take notes on one or two articles. Look for different theories about the way he died. What gear was he carrying? How well preserved were his remains? Do you believe he was murdered? What evidence is there to support that conclusion? Discuss your opinions with group members, and then write a group summary of your research.

BLOCK LETTER FORMAT

Using the block letter format, there are no indented lines.

Return address	77 Lincoln Avenue Wellesley, MA 02480
Date	May 10, 2002
Inside address	Dr. Rita Bennett Midland Hospital Senior Care Center 5000 Poe Avenue Dayton, OH 45414
Salutation	Dear Dr. Bennett:
Body of the letter	I am responding to your advertisement for a dietitian in the May 5 edition of the *New York Times*. I graduated from Boston University two years ago. Since graduation, I have been working at Brigham and Women's Hospital and have also earned additional certificates in nutritional support and diabetes education. I am interested in locating to the Midwest and will be happy to arrange for an interview at your convenience.
Complimentary close	Sincerely,
Signature	*Daniel Chin*
Typed name	Daniel Chin

INDENTED LETTER FORMAT

Using the indented format, the return address, the date, and the closing appear at the far right side of the paper. The first line of each paragraph is also indented.

Return address   77 Lincoln Avenue
                                                        Wellesley, MA 02480

Date   May 15, 2002

Inside address   Dr. Rita Bennett
                       Senior Care Center
                       5000 Poe Avenue
                       Dayton, OH 45414

Salutation   Dear Dr. Bennett:

Body of the   It was a pleasure to meet you and learn more about the
letter   programs offered at the Senior Care Center. I appreciate
                       your taking time out to show me around and introduce
                       me to the staff.

                           I am excited about the possibility of working at the
                       Senior Care Center and I look forward to talking with
                       you again soon.

Complimentary
close   Sincerely,

Signature   *Daniel Chin*

Typed name   Daniel Chin

DOCUMENTATION

College instructors usually require one of three formats (APA, Chicago, or MLA) to document the information you use in research papers and essays. The following pages compare and contrast the highlights of these three styles.

APA Style (American Psychological Association style)

1. **General Endnote Format**

    Title the page "References." Double-space the page and arrange the names alphabetically by authors' last names, the date in parentheses, followed by the rest of the information about the publication.

2. **Citation for a Single Author**

    Moore, Thomas. (1992). *The Care of the Soul.* New York: HarperPerennial.

3. **Citation for Multiple Authors**

    List the last names first followed by initials and use the "&" sign before the last author.
    Spinosa, C., Flores, F., & Dreyfus, H.L. (1997). *Disclosing New Worlds: Entrepreneurship, Democratic Action, and the Cultivation of Solidarity.* Cambridge: MIT Press.

4. **Citation for an Editor as Author**

    Wellwood, J. (Ed.). (1992). *Ordinary Magic: Everyday Life as a Spiritual Path.* Boston: Shambhala Publications.

5. **Citation for an Article in a Periodical**

    List the author, last name first, the year and month (and day if applicable) of the publication. Then list the title of the article (not underlined), the name of the publication (followed by the volume number if there is one) and the page number or numbers.
    Gibson, S. (2001, November). Hanging Wallpaper. *This Old House.* 77.

6. **Citation of On-line Materials**

    Provide enough information so that readers can find the information you refer to.
    Try to include the date on the posting, the title, the original print source (if any), a description of where you found the information, and the date you found the material.
    Arnold, W. (April 26, 2002). "Bogdanovich again mines Hollywood lore for 'Cat's Meow.'" (Movie Review) *Seattle Post-Intelligencer.* Retrieved May 1, 2002 on the World Wide Web: http://seattlepi.nwsource.com/printer2/index.asp?ploc=b

7. **General In-text Citation Format**

    Include three pieces of information: the last name of the author or authors of the work cited in the Endnotes, the year of publication, and the page(s) you refer to.
    (Moore, 1992, p. 7).
    (See items 1 and 2 above for related endnote entries.)

Chicago Style (from *The Chicago Manual of Style*)

1. **General Endnote Format**

   Title the page "Notes." Double-space the page. Number and indent the first line of each entry. Arrange the names alphabetically by authors' last names and use full names, not initials. Include page references at the end of the entry.

2. **Citation for a Single Author**

   Thomas Moore, *The Care of the Soul* (New York: HarperPerennial, 1992), 7–9.

3. **Citation for Multiple Authors**

   Charles Spinosa, Ferdinand Flores, and Hubert L. Dreyfus, *Disclosing New Worlds: Entrepreneurship, Democratic Action, and the Cultivation of Solidarity* (Cambridge: MIT Press, 1997), 66.

4. **Citation for an Editor as Author**

   Wellwood, J., ed. 1992. *Ordinary Magic: Everyday Life as Spiritual Path.* Boston: Shambhala Publications.

5. **Citation for an Article in a Periodical**

   List the author, last name first, the year of the publication. Then put the title of the article (not underlined), the name of the publication, the month, and the page number or numbers.

   Gibson, S. 2001. November. Hanging Wallpaper. *This Old House* November, 77.

6. **Citation of On-line Materials**

   Number and indent each entry and provide enough information so that readers can find the information you refer to. Try to include the author (first name first), the date on the posting (in parentheses), the title, the original print source (if any), a description of where you found the information, the URL, and the date you found the material (in parentheses).

   1. William Arnold, (April 26, 2002). "Bogdanovich again mines Hollywood lore for 'Cat's Meow'." (Movie Review) *Seattle Post-Intelligencer.* The World Wide Web: <http://seattlepi.nwsource.com/printer2/index.asp?ploc=b> (May 1, 2002)

7. **General In-text Citation Format**

   Number all in-text notes. The first time you cite a work within the text, use all the information as shown in 2. above. When citing the same work again, include only the last name of the author or authors and the page or pages you refer to.

   12. Moore, 8.

   (See items 1 and 2 above for related endnote entries.)

MLA Style (Modern Language Association style)

1. General Endnote Format

    Title the page "Works Cited." Double-space the page and arrange the names alphabetically by authors' last names, followed by the rest of the information about the publication as shown below.

2. Citation for a Single Author

    Moore, Thomas. *The Care of the Soul.* New York: HarperPerennial, 1992.

3. Citation for Multiple Authors

    List the last names first followed by full first names.

    Spinosa, Charles, Flores, Ferdinand, and Dreyfus, Hubert L. *Disclosing New Worlds: Entrepreneurship, Democratic Action, and the Cultivation of Solidarity.* Cambridge: MIT Press, 1997.

4. Citation for an Editor as Author

    Wellwood, John, ed. *Ordinary Magic: Everyday Life as Spiritual Path.* Boston: Shambhala Publications, 1992.

5. Citation for an Article in a Periodical

    List the author (last name first) the title of the article (using quotation marks), the title of the magazine (with no period), the date (followed by a colon), and the page number.

    Gibson, S. "Hanging Wallpaper." *This Old House* November 2001: 77.

6. Citation of On-line Materials

    Provide enough information so that readers can find the information you refer to. Try to include the date on the information, the title, the original print source (if any), the date you found the material, and the URL (if possible).

    Arnold, W. (April 26, 2002). "Bogdanovich again mines Hollywood lore for 'Cat's Meow'." (Movie Review) *Seattle Post-Intelligencer.* Retrieved April 26, 2002 on the World Wide Web: http://seattlepi.nwsource.com/printer2/index.asp?ploc=b

7. General In-text Citation Format

    Do not number entries. When citing a work listed in the "Works Cited" section, include only the last name of the author and the page or pages you refer to.

    (Moore 7–8).

    (See items 1 and 2 above for related endnote entries.)

INDEX OF KEY WORDS AND PHRASES

TECHNOLOGY-INTERNET

TOPICS